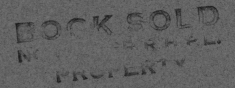

SONGS ON BRONZE

# SONGS ON BRONZE

## The Greek Myths Made Real

NIGEL SPIVEY

*faber and faber*

First published in 2005
by Faber and Faber Limited
3 Queen Square London WC1N 3AU

Typeset by Faber and Faber Ltd
Printed in England by Mackays of Chatham, plc

A CIP record for this book
is available from the British Library

ISBN 0–571–21541–6

2  4  6  8  10  9  7  5  3  1

On Saturday, July 30, Dr Johnson and I took a sculler at the Temple-stairs, and set out for Greenwich. I asked him if he really thought a knowledge of the Greek and Latin languages an essential requisite to a good education. JOHNSON. 'Most certainly, Sir; for those who know them have a very great advantage over those who do not. Nay, Sir, it is wonderful what a difference learning makes upon people even in the common intercourse of life, which does not appear to be much connected with it.' 'And yet, (said I) people go through the world very well, and carry on the business of life to good advantage, without learning.' JOHNSON. 'Why, Sir, that may be true in cases where learning cannot possibly be of any use; for instance, this boy rows us as well without learning, as if he could sing the song of Orpheus to the Argonauts, who were the first sailors.' He then called to the boy, 'What would you give, my lad, to know about the Argonauts?' 'Sir (said the boy), I would give what I have.' Johnson was much pleased with his answer, and we gave him a double fare.

Boswell, Life of Johnson: entry for 1763

# CONTENTS

# CONTENTS

# PRELUDE

# ORPHEUS IN LOVE

Eurydice was a girl born to the company of dryads, the spirits of woodlands and fields. So there was nothing she liked better than to hitch up her skirts and run barefoot through open countryside. And Orpheus, who loved her, was inclined to let her go. He was a poet: therefore it delighted him to see her move so free and fast. He doubted he could ever match her easy, flashing strides.

Just once he tried: kicked off his sandals, and followed in her trail. Within moments, he was howling in agony, hopping and clutching his heel. Eurydice dashed back to where he lay collapsed on the ground. She saw straightaway it was not the end of the world. Bending over, she seemed to plant a lingering kiss on the sole of her beloved's foot. With the tip of her tongue she located a thorn. Gently she extracted it, teasing it out with her teeth.

Orpheus swooned with relief. Eurydice held up the source of his pain: a tiny needle from the wild. Orpheus gasped in disbelief. 'Was that what brought me down?' She nodded. 'Ah,' he sighed. 'A lesson to us all.'

'How so?' she wondered.

'How Eros does his work,' Orpheus went on. 'We hardly see him, the little lord of love. Yet sure enough we feel his darts. Each one a spear thrust through the ribs.' He lay back in the grass and closed his eyes.

She knelt beside him, stroking his brow. 'Was that how it was with me?' she asked.

'With you . . . oh yes. With you, young Eros stabbed me very hard. A mortal wound – no less.'

Her fingers trembled in his hair. This man was a wondrous weaver of words, a ceaseless stitcher of songs; yet every utterance of his was like the stuff of truth. She deeply trusted him.

He sensed the hurt he had caused, and reached out for her hand. 'I only meant,' he said, 'that you – that you complete my life.'

Orpheus had a certain far-off sense: that one day, he would die for the love of his Eurydice. But he did not put it like that. Now she lay down with him, making what they craved: a meadowy hide, a refuge within sweet grass-stalks where they were joined and enclosed.

For a while they were silent, their heartbeats coming to merge. Eventually, she spoke.

'What makes me weep with wonder – is how I've always known you. Even when our lives were utterly apart: knowing you were there, somewhere; loving you before I ever saw you.'

'When I first set eyes on you,' said Orpheus, 'it wasn't love –'

Eurydice started; he touched her soothingly.

'– so much as recognition.'

She smiled, and settled her head on him.

'So,' she said. 'Tell me why.'

Orpheus did as he was told. It was, after all, his vocation – to tell things how and why.

'Well,' he began, 'hardly anyone knows this tale – but never mind. They say that, in the beginning, when the powers above chose to let us appear as playthings in their world, we mortals looked quite different from our present shape.'

Eurydice snugged deeper into his shoulder, to breathe him in the more.

'We were duplicate. Or at least, doubled in most respects. Two heads. Four arms. Four legs. A single torso, I think;

XII

but with two sets of genitals attached. Mostly these double humanoids had both male and female parts, but not all of them were like that: some were double man, some double woman. Those who wanted to reproduce did it automatically.'

He paused. Her head moved with his chest. Her eyes were closed. But she was quite awake.

'Like the crickets do,' she said. 'Not much fun.'

'Oh, but we were very happy that way. We went cartwheeling around, terribly pleased with ourselves. Too pleased for our own good. We thought there was nothing that we couldn't do. We thought we were simply divine. We planned to take heaven by storm.'

'Oh, did we?' cooed Eurydice.

'Yes. That was when the deities on Mount Olympus grew alarmed. They held a council, to discuss our turbulent behaviour. Almighty Zeus gave the order – to have us sliced in half. Cut us down to size. For a while he was tempted to get rid of us altogether; but then who would be left to worship him and the other gods? So it was that each of us was weakened by a drastic split. We were stitched up and rearranged, of course. Apollo did the surgery, and he did it as neatly as he could. But forever after we have suffered from the wound – left like tallies of our former selves. So it's deep in our nature, now, to roam in search of the missing part – our other half – to be fused as once we were.'

Orpheus clasped Eurydice as tightly as he could. 'Somewhat,' he hummed, 'like this.'

'It's nice,' said Eurydice. 'But I don't believe a word. Now tell us how it really was.'

'From the beginning?' said Orpheus.

'Anywhere,' murmured Eurydice. 'So long as it ends with us.'

'Very well.' Orpheus gathered his breath. *'Once upon a time* . . . '

XIII

# I

# AN EARLY CHILDHOOD
# OF THE WORLD

# OUT OF CHAOS

Once upon a time there was no Time.

It was a void without days, hours, or anything ticking by. No light shone, no dark fell, nothing moved – because there was nothing to move, nowhere to go. It was the empty, ageless state of Chaos.

No one can tell when Chaos began to grow into form. But no one can doubt what came with the growth. It was Eros: zero's opposite. The same force that rocks us at the knees: Eros, the divine ignition of the world.

A shape appeared in Chaos. Smooth, solid, hugely calm, this was Gaia – Mother Earth. Above Gaia there stretched a broad, wide-shouldered form. It was Ouranos – the Sky.

As such they might have stayed there, Gaia and Ouranos, apart for all time – if Eros had not stirred, and loosed his darts.

Ouranos gazed on Gaia, and marvelled at her loveliness. His heart drummed hard with desire. Ouranos lowered himself down, on top of Gaia, and caressed her flesh. He made a gully where he could insert himself in Gaia's pliant clay. Once he thrust himself inside, she was never so smooth again. Ouranos heaved and sweated there. He cast his seed and rolled away for slumber while Gaia stayed awake.She yearned for her lover. He came to her again, and again – swooping as Eros ruled. Meanwhile Gaia swelled with the seed Ouranos left. Her belly grew and grew until, with a heaven-searching howl, Gaia pushed out what was inside her.

It came out as a surge, rushing into eddies and waves. It was a burly, eager thing. It was the Ocean, and it showed its strength with a roar.

Ouranos looked down upon Gaia, nursing the noisy child. In the tides and tows of young Ocean, Ouranos glimpsed sinews of himself, which pleased him. But Ouranos was jealous too. He had folded Gaia in his arms. He had caused her to gasp and smile. Now she crooned over this Ocean playing in her lap. What was this splashy toy to her?

He puffed himself up. He descended again. 'Love me,' he boomed, gripping Gaia hard.

Once more Gaia was swollen with his seed. Once more she broke open, issuing forth a shiny, round-faced thing, whose name would be Helios. Gaia fondled the golden creature, and again Ouranos was petulant.

'Give that thing to me,' he demanded. 'I made it. I want it.' Ouranos gathered Helios up into his own high place in the sky, and kept him there.

Gaia moaned to see Helios gone so far from her. So long as she could see him, beaming, she felt comforted and warm. But if ever Helios went out of her sight, then Gaia felt the ache of his loss. She would shiver and weep.

Gaia was placid and good. Ouranos, always around and above her, could lay himself down as he liked. So he did. But he no longer stroked her surfaces, nor whispered how lovely she was. He made his entry, left his sperm, and ignored her when she swelled. Gaia gave birth to Night, packed with dreams; to the Moon, Selene, who is Night's lantern; to the Hesperides, the swaying girls of twilight; and to Aurora, the Dawn, with her jug of silvery dew. Still Ouranos pounded, still the offspring increased. These last were large, lumbering figures, the Titans. Big strivers they were, roaming widely, full of ambition and grandiose dreams.

But the youngest of these Titans stayed close to Gaia. His name was Kronos. He was more thoughtful than the others, more ready with words; but weaker and punier too – a Titanic runt. Ouranos mocked Kronos as soon as he was born. The boy could do nothing that redeemed him in his father's eyes. Once, Ouranos found Kronos playing in a pit of sand that Gaia had given to the boy. Kronos had a fistful of grains, which he let trickle into a mound; he sat, gleeful, surrounded by such mounds.

'Look, Father,' said Kronos, as the sand ran through his fingers. 'This will make an hour.'

'An hour?' Ouranos sneered. 'What's an hour good for?'

Scornful Ouranos kicked and huffed the mounds of sand, spreading them as deserts across the globe. Thereafter, Kronos would hide himself whenever Ouranos bore down on Gaia's weary form. From his hiding place, Kronos saw how his mother was seized. He witnessed Gaia's wince and shudder; observed her sparse pleasure, and then her lonely distress. When Ouranos hauled himself away, Kronos would creep back to his mother's lap.

Mother and son plotted revenge.

'An hour,' said Kronos to Gaia. 'An hour is how long he sleeps down here. It will take less, much less, to do what he deserves.'

Gaia dug down to what was needed for their plan: a jagged edge of flint. Kronos kept it hidden by his side. When Ouranos next dropped upon Gaia and began his straddling, Kronos lurked with this sickle in his grasp. When Ouranos gained his release, rolling off to rest by Gaia's warmth, Kronos sneaked forward. For a moment he looked, half-fondly, upon the face of his father, sprawled and snoring, wearing a satisfied smile.

But Gaia was not smiling. She had suffered too many hurts from this slumberous form. She nodded to Kronos, who raised his curving blade. He took one swipe, and another. Ouranos first jerked, still sleeping, then snapped stark awake in astonished pain. Shaking his head, Ouranos put his hand to his groin and gaped: it was a stub, pulsing black and red. Ouranos shrieked for what was gone. But Kronos was away, sprinting with his prize.

Where the hacked-off genitals of Ouranos dripped blood, that blood created crucibles of cosmic anger, the boiling volcanoes of the world. And as he ran, Kronos heard his father scream a curse that never left his ears. The curse damned Kronos, for all the endless hours there were, to live in fear of what his loins produced.

Ouranos retired to fade and die among the heavens that were his element.

Aghast and sickened, Kronos hurled the bloodied fragments of his father into Ocean's swirling waters.

It was an ugly act, deserved or not. But Eros triumphs over shame. Thrown into a cool deep sea, the testicle-sacks of Ouranos fizzed with energy. Their store of sperm spilled out, and came foaming up like surf, as Aphrodite rose from the frothing seed.

What was left of Ouranos was Love.

# PROMETHEUS AND PANDORA

So Kronos was saddled with a curse: that his own offspring would be the death of him. He took it seriously. By his partner, Rhea, he fathered several children; but as each one appeared, Kronos grabbed the baby in a welter of tears and rage, cramming the newly issued bodies into his mouth; nearly choking, he swallowed them whole. He was unstoppable.

Or so it seemed. In her final pregnancy, Rhea contrived to deliver her child unseen, within the recess of a cave. The boy was Zeus, whom she left tucked up in a corner; meanwhile she took a small rock, swaddled it in rags, and emerged into the daylight cooing and cuddling the effigy to her breast. As she expected, Kronos tore the bundle away from her, and gulped it down. This time his stomach protested, and he began to retch.

'What else do you expect?' cried Rhea. 'You castrated your father; you devour your children.'

Disgusted with himself, Kronos vomited forth not only the stone, but the other babies too. They came squirming out. Rhea, triumphantly, gathered them up, and made off back to the place where she had hidden the infant Zeus. There she nurtured her tenderlings upon the milk of deathlessness. They were to outmatch the Titans. They were to be divine.

Hestia was one. Unobtrusive, demure, she grew to be the

guardian of hearth and homeliness. Another was Hera, in time the mistress of fertile motherhood. Also Demeter, who was destined to be matron of all that blooms and thrives. Of Rhea's salvaged brood, however, most prompt to rise and jostle for seats of godly rule were three sharp-elbowed lads. First was Zeus, who chose the heavens for his realm, and took possession of all clouds that gather there; thunder made his anger, lightning bolts his weaponry. Second came Poseidon, who marshalled the seas, and all the songless tribes of fish that flicker through the brine. Last was Hades. Now Hades was not like the others. Zeus was ample and open; for all that his temper could be fierce, he was by nature broad-minded and with a gaze that took in everything. Poseidon was impetuous, easily raised to shake the earth with his sudden fits of pride; but, equally, he might send breezes flowing round the torrid earth, and make halcyon days when even the flashing kingfisher may float with her brood on the surface of the deep. But Hades – Hades kept a single mood: sullen, shadowed, chewing everything over. Hades had no sooner entered the world than he retired from it. He claimed his element down below, in the guts of the earth. He became lord of the land that is not land, ringed by black waters that have no source nor end, the coiling River Styx. It is the Underworld – which is where, sooner or later, we all must drop: like leaves.

So the three boys of Rhea set themselves up. As for their father, they would have set upon and ousted him, as he had his father before; but Kronos saved them the trouble. He withdrew. Dimly it is remembered that he was granted a sort of mellow exile in the land of Italy, where mortals later worshipped him as Saturn, and his reign was acclaimed as a Golden Age for men and beasts alike. In any case, Kronos was gone. Now it was the self-appointed task of Zeus to settle the elements; to govern a cosmos that worked.

There are nipples on the earth that end in clouds. Zeus made his bastion on one of these, the snowy peak of Mount Olympus in Macedonia. Around him he mustered his company. There were his siblings, naturally. Of the women, Demeter was unstinting and good-willed, and Hestia wanted no more than to kindle universal happiness, so he could count on their support; but Zeus knew that his prickly sister Hera would not abide to be less than a queen. He proposed she join his reign, as consort; all honour to him should therefore be hers as well. Hera frowned, but she did not refuse.

This would never be an easy union. Zeus sought his passion elsewhere, while Hera kept up a pretence of married bliss. By other partners Zeus produced Hermes, swift purveyor of news; Apollo, the god who shines and sees afar; Apollo's twin Artemis, the huntress who finds blood with her arrows and whip; and Dionysos, lord of ecstasy. The only son that Hera bore by Zeus was Ares, the bristling god that no one loves. Provoker of clashes, spiller of blood, Ares forever carried with him the quarrelsome taint of his parents. His lullaby was nothing but shouts, yells, recriminations.

Once, to punish her husband, Hera coupled elsewhere. She gave birth to an awkward but powerful boy, who showed a rare gift for putting things together and taking them apart: Hephaistos. Zeus regarded the child with suspicion at first. At the height of one quivering argument with Hera, Zeus seized Hephaistos and flung him through the skies. Hephaistos crashed heavily to earth. He came back not only awkward but markedly lame. Then Zeus took pity on this bastard son, and gave him a place on Olympus: a workshop, a furnace, and whatever materials and instruments were needed to supply the marvels of this ingenious youth. Still Hera smouldered, chiding Zeus for his lack of self-control. Zeus withdrew into a dark sulk, accumulating clouds around him. When he emerged he was clutching his head.

'Who, pray, shall soothe our noble lord?' asked Hera, cuttingly.

'Hephaistos,' groaned Zeus. 'Call him to me. Then see,' he snarled to Hera, 'how I control all things.'

Hephaistos hobbled along, lugging his toolbag. Zeus was squeezing his temples in pain. 'Now enjoy yourself,' he grimaced to Hephaistos. 'Go on, lad. Aim for the cranium. Strike it hard.'

Hephaistos looked to Hera, who only shrugged. Zeus sat on his throne, and gripped its gleaming lion's paws. 'Get on with it!' he barked. Hephaistos selected a mallet, measured his distance, and dealt a sharp emphatic blow. For a moment Zeus fell forward with the force of the crack; then his head tipped back – a smile of relief spread across his face. His skull was split – but without mess or pain. Instead, what issued forth was a goddess. She rose tall and imperious, brandishing a spear; with one leap she was in the lap of Zeus. His wound healed immediately, and he lost no time in crowing to his wife:

'To Zeus,' he declared, ' Zeus, from Zeus: a daughter. Zeus gives her strength – with softness; wisdom – with docility. Zeus names her: Athena.'

Hera turned on her heels. She would not be beaten for long.

Meanwhile, Zeus had other battles on his hands. There were Titans at large in the world. Most were dull-witted, and Zeus soon had them either extinct or under control. One was called Atlas: Zeus merely harnessed that Titan's enormous shoulders to hold up the weight of heaven. But others were more wily, and taxed the mind of Zeus – none more so than Prometheus.

Prometheus was born of Gaia, Mother Earth. He was witness to the triple division by which Rhea's boys had assigned

to themselves the skies, the seas, and the sombre under-
ground. Prometheus settled for less – a continent or so. He
lived there quietly enough with a simpleton brother of his,
called Epimetheus, the two of them foraging day by day. Still,
Prometheus tinkered with making a realm of his own. One
day, delving in some riverbeds, he came across a strange and
mobile sort of clay. He grabbed a lump and began to knead it
into a shape. Legs, arms, joints and all. There – a fan of nimble
fingers. There – a bobbing head. And there – a phallus craving
friction. It was a mannikin, a toy, but it was immediately
endearing to Prometheus. He lifted it up, and crooned his
breath into its bold little torso. The trick worked: Prometheus
set his figure on the ground, and watched it toddle, run, scam-
per and hide. In a similar way he amused himself by moulding
other small things to scuttle and rove around – things with
snouts and trunks and spikes and humps, all sorts of company
for the tiny man. His brother Epimetheus was delighted at
how these creatures moved and busied themselves, yet
Prometheus was not quite satisfied. He gave his manchild an
affectionate poke.

'Now what you need,' he said, 'is something more. Some
element that sets you apart, that gives you an edge above the
rest.'

Prometheus knew just what he wanted, and where he could
find it. Grasping the hollow stalk of a giant fennel plant, he
crept up to Olympus one afternoon when Zeus was out adventuring. And there it was, lodged in the misty heights of the
home of Zeus: a scalded cauldron, filled to its brim with lightning bolts. Quick – as a flash – Prometheus snatched up a single electrified strand, slid it into his fennel tube, and made
away, blowing his fingers.

Prometheus was halfway down the slopes of Olympus
when he met the returning Zeus.

Wise Zeus looked him up and down. 'Out for a hike in the hills?' he enquired.

Prometheus nodded hastily. Behind his back, the fennel wand glowed in his hands.

Zeus sniffed the air. 'Odd,' he said. 'Faint smell of burning. You notice it?'

'Not at all,' said Prometheus. 'Excuse me,' he coughed. 'Must be pressing on.'

It was a relieved and blistering Prometheus who reached his home camp with the stolen fire. Straightaway his brother and the little man began to gather brushwood and twigs. Soon smoke was rising up from the land of scuttling things.

Zeus noticed it, of course. As Prometheus knew he would. But Prometheus had a plan to appease the eventual rage of Zeus. He organized a celebration. He and stolid Epimetheus stoked up the fire, and over the flames they roasted one of the stout oxen that browsed in the pastures nearby. When the beast was cooked, Prometheus divided it up. To one side he displayed a pile of blood-glazed steaks. Then he gathered up the trimmings – the bones, the gristle and the offal – and wrapped them neatly in a shiny package of animal lard.Then he called for Zeus to join the feast.

'See, my lord,' he declared, 'how we honour our superiors. For you we have slaughtered the finest of our herd. Take the portion that pleases your highness.'

Epimetheus sniggered as Zeus took the parcel of fat. But Zeus was not fooled. His fury broke. Zeus seized Prometheus, pushed him up against a crag and pinioned the Titan fast. By day Prometheus writhed under the parching blaze of the sun; by night there was no respite, for Zeus sent a huge-winged eagle to probe the exposed body of Prometheus; to rummage with talons and beak for the Titan's very entrails. And if that were not ordeal enough, Zeus allowed the gizzards of

Prometheus to freshen and renew themselves – keeping the eagle keen.

While Prometheus suffered for his raid of fire, his diminutive man enjoyed its use and warmth. Nuggets of ore were plucked from bedrocks, and forged into hammers and ploughs. Zeus watched the creature's industry with a gentle smile. Was this the sum of the powers of Prometheus – this petty, two-legged automaton, so earnestly trying to thrive on the crust of the earth? More intrigued than angry, Zeus decided to have some fun of his own. He paid a visit to Hephaistos, describing what he required, and looked on as the smith god quickly took up some slippery paste and began to knead and shape it. Zeus invited his fellow divines along, to share in the game of creation. When it was done, Zeus went to the place where Prometheus hung, wrecked and subdued.

'Enough,' said Zeus. 'My temper has cooled. I have a surprise for you. A peace-offering.'

He unchained Prometheus from the outcrop, and brought him down to the grassy balm of a soft meadow. In the midst of this field there was a small figure, standing utterly still upon a base of polished marble. Prometheus gaped. The figure was about the same size as his man, and made of similar matter. But the detail, the finish, the delicacy of this piece – they stole his breath.

She was crowned with columbines and new-grown herbs; swathed in clinging robes of the finest fabric, with a tracery of gold braided throughout. Her hair came down to her shoulders; her form was pert and glowing and fine; her face fixed in a shy glance of impossible allure.

At her feet stood a wooden chest with a bronze clasp.

'Well?' said Zeus.

'Perfect!' whispered Prometheus.

Zeus gave an exclamation of mocking self-reproach.

'But not so!' he cried. 'One more gift – I almost forgot.'

Zeus grinned, leaned down to the statuette, and sent a puff of his breath over the garlanded head.

Instantly, her cheeks dimpled with a smile and her eyes came alight. She tossed her glossy hair, and stepped down from the pedestal. Slowly at first, but with exquisite poise, she started to dance. The actions started with her dainty ankles. Then she extended her arms, and swayed her hips; for a moment, even Zeus was amazed. Ingenious Hephaistos – how did he do it? And the others too, how forthcoming they had been: Apollo had given her this musical sense – and who knew what else the Olympians had contributed, stored in the wooden dowry-box . . .

'She has a name,' announced Zeus: 'Pandora, which means "All-Endowed"; or, if you prefer, "All-Giving". Go on,' he urged. 'Take her. Let her partner and comfort that brave little mud-baked toy of yours.'

Prometheus shrugged. He had not been deprived of his sense of suspicion. 'Really,' he said. 'I don't deserve so much. I couldn't.'

In the pause that ensued, both Zeus and Prometheus became aware of a third presence. It was shambling Epimetheus. He was nodding, mesmerized, as Pandora danced and laughed and sang. A vast happiness had spread across his placid face.

'No, brother, no –' groaned Prometheus.

But already good-hearted Epimetheus had stepped forward. He tenderly bowed to the twinkling girl.

'Yours,' said Zeus, 'for keeps.'

Epimetheus took Pandora's hand, to escort his livesome doll away. Prometheus gloomily joined them.

'Wait,' called Zeus. He held up the wooden casket that had stood at Pandora's feet. 'Don't forget this. Take great care of it.'

Prometheus halted with dismay. But Epimetheus grabbed the box, and weighed it up. It seemed both vacant and yet the heaviest load in the world. He tucked it cheerfully under his arm. For all its heft, it was a compact container; it surely held nothing very substantial. He would open it later.

For a long while, Pandora's box stayed shut, and out of sight. Pandora herself was marvel enough. Even Prometheus, who could not believe that Zeus ever intended him any kindness, grudgingly accepted that Pandora brought them nothing but delight. Athena had granted her an elastic capacity for care and thoughtfulness towards others. Hestia had graced her with the daily-practised arts of making a home. And Aphrodite – fair Aphrodite had bestowed upon Pandora powers to arouse the longings of Eros: a most delicious tyranny.

For the darling creature of Prometheus she was a natural mate. They came together under Aphrodite's spell, and produced tiny, screaming replicas of themselves. The earth was, after all, a spacious habitat; great tracts of it were occupied by no one, save here and there the odd clumsy Titan, or isolated camps of surly Giants, the Titans' lesser cousins. To create a happy community in the fertile garden of the world – what could be better than that? Everything seemed to be flourishing here, with these groundlings and their settlement of thatched huts. The families multiplied, but there was food in abundance for all. Cows came and gave their udders to be milked; the forests were hampers of honey and berries and nuts. No one thought to mark off property with fences; still less to defend it with blades and spears.

One evening – years later – as he gazed proudly over the contented cluster of households that Pandora had spawned, Epimetheus remembered the box.

Vaguely he recalled carrying it home; vaguely he recalled that Prometheus had put it away for safe-keeping. What was it that Zeus had said – Take great care of it? But had he done so? Did he even know where it was?

Anxiously now, Epimetheus sought out his brother. That box, entrusted to them by Zeus – was it lost? At first Prometheus denied all knowledge of it. Then, seeing the dismay engraved upon his brother's kindly brow, Prometheus admitted: yes, he had hidden the box. Why? Epimetheus demanded. Because, said Prometheus – it might be dangerous. Dangerous how? Epimetheus pursued. Just – well, dangerous, said Prometheus, aware that his own fears and premonitions about the casket had paled. But anyway, he swiftly added – what more did they need in their lives? What on earth was there that those creatures lacked?

Epimetheus remained disconsolate. He sloped around, gnawed by remorse and curiosity. The box had come as part of Pandora. Might it hold something she ought to possess, by right? Then another thought occurred to him. Before Pandora arrived, he had been as happy as he imagined he could ever be. Then Pandora came and, amazingly, she had created even more happiness. What if her box carried the secrets of still further delight? As the days went by, Epimetheus grew increasingly obsessed by the box, and miserable for its return. Finally Prometheus yielded, and fetched it from its hiding place.

No sooner had Prometheus handed the box to his brother than he felt his old forebodings descend.

'Stay,' said Epimetheus excitedly. 'We'll open it together.'

Prometheus shook his head, and walked dubiously away. Within moments he knew that the latch on Pandora's box had been lifted. The skies became bruised and blotched; the wind picked up. Clouds hurried, piling on top of each other, with quick spits of lightning; all rolled along to a sound that Prometheus knew of old – the thunderous, ill-meaning laughter of Zeus. Prometheus looked back. Spiralling up from the place where he had left Epimetheus with Pandora's box there billowed a purple-black column, twisting and screeching over the land. Prometheus did not know what it carried in its vortex; only inklings hissed about him, of untold woes and worse.

> Rancour, cruelty, violence, terror, spite . . .
> pollution, corruption, poison, plague . . .
> loneliness, hatred,
> prejudice, greed . . .
> vanity, slander . . . vengefulness . . .
> failure, betrayal . . . insolence, indifference
> cheating, malice, mistrust . . .
> heartache, rejection . . . hunger, lies,
> setbacks, shoddiness, backbiting,
> envy, disaster,
> pain . . .

As this whirlwind screeched around his ears, Prometheus threw himself to the ground and covered his face. When at last it died away – almost as suddenly as it had arisen – he picked himself up, and slowly retraced his steps.

He came by the village of humankind. It seemed not to have been flattened by the gale. But it was not intact either. Smoke came from two of the huts, reduced to a scatter of brands; a third was blazing.

There were bodies strewn around. Some were charred; but others were broken and pierced.

Peering closer, Prometheus saw that a few of his little folk stood around, slapping their heads. Their mouths were squared in howls, bewailing what was before them: an infant and mother, laid out lifeless in the dust.

In one area, men were crouched over anvils, beating metal into spear-points; while in another part, they were busy chipping flint into barbed arrowheads.

Prometheus watched them; but they did not notice him. Their faces were determined. Their hands moved deftly in the industry of hate.

Prometheus plodded on. He found Epimetheus. To blame him was unnecessary: he was hunched over, rocking to and fro, blubbing tears as big as puddles.

Epimetheus clutched to himself a limp form. The dangling dainty ankles told whose it was. Epimetheus was beyond comfort's reach. For a long while the two Titan brothers simply sat side by side, speechless.

They knew their world would never be the same.

Pandora's box lay where it had been dropped. Eventually, Prometheus picked it up. It seemed to have nothing inside. Yet it also seemed not quite empty. Whatever dread it had held, there was something else besides.

The clouds lifted. Sunlight returned to the glades.

Prometheus shook the box. What he heard was slight, but it was not Nothing.

It was the rattle of Hope.

# DEMETER AND PERSEPHONE

The Giants were minor cousins of the Titans; yet big sprawling brutes all the same. Insolent lumps, they launched a siege of Mount Olympus. Their only weapons were whatever came to hand – but they had very big hands. Where they scooped up clods of soil, they left valleys. The rocks with which they pelted the gods remained as outcrops and hills. The battle caused upheaval in every direction. Zeus flung down his thunderbolts, pinning the Giants to the surface of the earth. He rallied the other Olympians too. Apollo let fly with arrows in clusters to darken the sky. Artemis, his sister, strode into combat with a pack of mastiffs and panthers at her heel; to see her pets rip sinews apart was something that made this stern goddess laugh. But the most damage was done by Poseidon. The Giants provoked Poseidon to his deepest rage. He boiled and twisted from below, thrusting his floodwaters high and hard and without respite. Most of the Giants sank to a choking end as seawaves invaded their lungs. Dragged down to the ocean floor, there they lie: the troughs and reefs that mariners still fear.

To this day there is hardly a soul in the world that has not some far-off recollection of the terror in that mêlée. Of the miniature beings spawned by Prometheus – those left to bicker and fight after the opening of Pandora's box – just one couple survived. Their names were Deucalion and Pyrrha. They built themselves a boat, and bobbed about until the anger of Poseidon died. They had a son called Hellen, from whom all the Hellenic tribes descend. Other peoples remember a Flood, but with different names; some talk of a grand salvage of animals too.

Whoever they were, life was never to be for them as it once had been for the creatures of Prometheus: fruits and plenty tipping in from all around – unkept cattle brimming milk – a land not scarred with boundaries. All that was gone. Instead it was sweat, and aching limbs.

*Mouths to feed? Then clear the trees. Make a plough-beam of the oak. Harness oxen to it, turn earth into clods, sow the furrows. Tend the grain till it is bearded and tall. Cut it down. Thrash out its chaff. Grind the kernels into flour, store the precious dust . . .*

That was the new order for mortals on earth: hard graft for good return.

And even then it was a very precarious concession.

*. . . squint into the powerful sun and pray it does not scorch; hoard rain in cisterns and hope against a flood . . .*

To dig, to plant; to hoe, prune, trim, cut, bundle and stack – all these are useless labours, without Demeter's aid.

Demeter, daughter of Rhea. Zeus, son of Kronos. It is best not to press for intimate details: let us simply say that of Zeus and Demeter a girl was born. Her name was Persephone.

Demeter is the goddess who fosters produce and fruitfulness across the earth. But, naturally, she reserved special pride for her very own. If ever a child was the apple of her mother's eye, it was Persephone. Persephone shone. Wherever she went, she scattered radiance, a beaming out to all: the polar opposite of hatefulness and dark. By itself, that charm might have been resistible. But the warmth was not in pious isolation. How Persephone's hips joined her waist was a mystery many men would have dreamed to explore. Her breasts were like promontories of a longed-for land. And her gait was sheer dilemma: it swung so pleasingly from innocence to guile. This from a girl not yet sixteen.

Persephone brought delight everywhere: even where it was scarcely welcome.

Such as in the view of Hades.

Hades, we have already observed, was not much like his brothers Zeus and Poseidon. He maintained none of their ever-roving interest in pink-thighed girls and boys. He stayed in his own dank allotment, and waited for pale and spectral visitors from above; of which he had, after all, a steady supply. Just sometimes he wandered upwards, to survey life's brevity and puff. It was then – in the hour of the tallest shadows – that Hades caught sight of Persephone.

She was with girlfriends. They were preparing for the night; unbraiding each other's tresses; laughing among themselves. At any other time, Hades would have shrugged, and returned below. But now he lingered by the sliding sun, an unseen spy on this group. It was not the group that caused him to stay – just one of them: the edge of her neck, the shake of her hair; a single voice rising pure and high above the rest.

As Hades stared at the girl his knees began to melt. There was a tremor in his stance that was entirely new to him.

Eros was the novelty.

Hades tottered below and brooded. For days he lurked in his Underworld, and waited for this weakness to pass. On the contrary, it settled more deeply upon him: a torment stoked by solitude. There was nothing to do but rise again to the upper air – and catch the sight once more.

He endeavoured to watch her alone. The opportunity came, because Persephone was her mother's daughter. Not a day went by when she did not sway through the grasslands to sample the blooms that were there. She took a wicker basket, humming along. What had she to fear? Snapdragon, foxglove, deadnettle, furze?

Hades decided that she must be his wife.

So he who rules where spirits end is not quite granite-hard. Hades, whose judgement for mortals allows no appeal, was struck fair and true by Eros, and he yielded. Then he strove to make it a decent surrender – madness with dignity. He knew there could be no courtship. One sight of him and Persephone would scream. Still, he would do the thing properly, so far as he could. To plead the permission of this girl's hand in marriage, he went to her father.

In truth, Zeus rarely saw this daughter of his. But it was even more seldom that he had a visit, on Olympus, from the lord of the beyond. There was no such thing as a mere social call from that baleful presence. So Zeus welcomed his brother – and would-be son-in-law.

Hades explained his desire directly, honestly – and with a passionate intensity that Zeus would never have imagined of him. Zeus tried some fraternal banter in reply.

'No,' he said, chuckling. 'I can't allow this. How can you possibly know what you want, when this is the first time of wanting? Take my advice. Try out the field. The world is yours. You could have anything – nymph, stripling, beast. Go on. Roam around. Compare; contrast.'

Hades stared at him: not uncomprehending – but with the blank, unhappy gaze of one who is misunderstood.

'Well,' said Zeus, equally puzzled. 'What would you do – if I said no?'

Hades shrugged. 'We are undying, you and I?' he said.

'We are,' said Zeus.

'Without her,' said Hades, 'I would renounce it.'

Fool, thought Zeus. And you would.

'As you wish,' Zeus declared. 'Take her. See what she does for you. Embrace the untold joys of matrimony.'

As if on cue, there came a cry of anger down a corridor, followed by the scarcely mistakable sounds of Zeus' consort, Hera, delivering a tirade to some sobbing maidservant. Sharp smacks could be heard. Zeus winced. Then he smiled: for, again as if on signal, a slim young boy glided into the room. The boy was naked. He carried a tray bearing a pitcher of wine and two gold chalices. He set down the drinks, and smirked, as his shining loins were fondly stroked.

'This,' said Zeus, 'is my Ganymede: a mortal promoted to our deathless state. One day he was minding those absurd four-legged things that bleat and munch grass all day. The next, he was borne aloft to me upon an eagle's back. And why? Because, brother, he pleases me; and we please each other. You see? Compare; contrast.'

Zeus sighed; and allowed the youth to shimmer away.

'Frankly,' he said, 'I have, to date, more offspring than I can remember. Is that so very bad?'

Hades said nothing.

'Well,' said Zeus. 'Persephone is yours.' He paused. 'Perhaps,' he added, 'we won't tell her mother. Not just yet.'

Next day, Persephone came down to one of her favourite places: a meadow where she wandered singing, chorused by thousands of crickets. She halted among some of the blossoms she knew. A huge narcissus had sprung up here, its petals trumpeting loud and bold. It was a monster of a plant: she had never seen anything like it. Persephone stooped to finger the milky flowers, which for all their blaring brightness seemed so curiously pale and cold. She was momentarily absorbed. She did not hear the point when all the crickets stopped.

Nor she did know, clearly, what happened next. It was as if the ground were split by hundreds of hammering hoofbeats; everything flew entangled in a chariot's rapid clatter. She felt herself seized and pulled aboard; then dropping down, down, and deeper into a stale and sunless gloom.

Hades tried to be soft. But it was not the force of his grip that hurt Persephone. It was the piercing, tight-fast cold.

And the shadow that had no light behind.

Can mothers sense these things from afar? Demeter, at home, was aware of a lurch and a tug. She started a scream; then, ashamed, let herself laugh. A child, as she so often reasoned, always came to its parents on loan. However precious her daughter, she must be allowed to explore. One day, after all, Persephone would go; and that time lay not far off. But today, said Demeter to herself – today, without doubt, she will be back, as always, brimming with stories and flowers.

There is such a thing as mild panic. An hour or two late? Not to worry. All sorts of possible hitches. Get on with some minor jobs. Supper will keep. Still. One is hinged to a window, or hangs by the door. Of course all is well. Of course it must be. Of course it could . . . It might be yet . . . Why, any moment now . . .

So Demeter awaited her daughter's return. Dusk deepened into night, and fireflies began to twinkle in the olive groves. Then, with arms folded, crooning the name and all its playful variants, Demeter went searching for Persephone. She walked through all the flower-crowded fields, by every stream and spinney that was known to the girl; she called down every dale and rise for Persephone, Persephone. There was no response. Creatures joined the hunt: snuffling badgers, big-eyed owls. But no sign of Persephone.

It was quite as if the earth had just swallowed her up.

And it was the agony of not knowing that even peaceful Demeter could not bear. Her moaning rose to the skies. Other deities knew full well where Persephone was kept. But at dawn it was only Helios who could bring himself to whisper to Demeter of what he had seen the previous day, under his burnishing gaze. Angry, but half-relieved, Demeter hurried straight to the top of Olympus.

'Back,' insisted Demeter to a cowering Zeus. 'You let her go down there; you, now, bring her back!'

Zeus tried oily persuasion. Hades, he said, was really not as he seemed. In his own way, Hades would prove an admirable helpmate for Persephone. Agreed, her life would be less than a festival of mirth. But she could depend on a husband who had (continued Zeus, somewhat nervously) many virtues. Why, he was solid, reliable and loyal. Attentive, regular, upright, fair . . .

'And cold. And dark. And his face never cracked by a smile,' added Demeter, bitterly. 'While all that *she* loves lies under sun and stars. So. Let her return.'

Then Zeus turned adamant. 'I gave my word,' he said. 'The girl is in good hands. Now go. And be calm about this.'

Demeter went. And, in a sense, she was obedient to Zeus. She was becalmed. Her own and only child was gone. So she herself slid into listlessness. She lost her love of life.

Demeter was the sort of mother who always had something on the stove. She kept her kitchen as the household's warm hub, stockaded with preserves, cuttings, tubs of basil, knotted garlic, peppers in dangling strips. Now it became cobwebbed and cool. The goddess herself, once so rosy and flushed, retired into her grief. Her cheeks hollowed, her shoulders sagged; her skin turned ashen grey.

It was then that the world learned just what it owed to Demeter.

At first toiling mortals put it down to bad luck. Seeds sown failed to sprout: time to drag out the mattocks and ploughshares and try over again. But as the days of Demeter's bereavement became weeks, the pattern of failure spread. Everything seemed eerily sterile. No buds poked out; not a plant advanced. All grass was parched, all ripeness stalled. What fruits there were went sour.

From the vantage of Olympus, no one saw this crisis sooner than Ganymede, Zeus' cup-bearing boy. Once a shepherd himself, Ganymede was quick to hear the troubled ewes, driven up to yet higher ground in hope of a few green tufts. He alerted his master, who cast his eyes over the scene below. Zeus saw the skeletal cattle and cankering fruits; the desperate little humans, scraping for handfuls of food; and he was duly perturbed. What had gone so amiss upon the fertile earth?

Zeus sought out Demeter. She was rocking herself in a chair. She was scarcely recognizable: unkempt and withdrawn.

'Glad I found you . . . ' he began.

Demeter shook her head. 'Me?' she mused, as if to herself. 'It's not *me* you need to find.'

Zeus got no more from her. He returned angrily to Olympus. Then Ganymede fetched out a huge sable coat, and Zeus braced himself to descend not only below, but beneath what was below: somewhere he had never taken himself, until now.

The god gave his valet a parting kiss. 'You know who's to blame for all this?' Zeus grumbled. Ganymede shrugged.

'Eros. Who else?'


But how, in all this, was Persephone herself? After the scuffle of abduction, and once Persephone understood that she had no way of escape, Hades kept his distance. He had asked what he could do to make her happy; but all she could sob was, *Leave me alone*. Which he tried to do. Already he had rooms set aside for her, appointed with every comfort. He looked in only to pledge his tenderness; and to assure her that, while she had been brought deep into the spirit world, it was not totally gloom and decay. Spirits came, as it were, from every walk of life.

She seemed inconsolable. Hades found among his teeming subjects a juggler – a springy Nubian lad, whose performing career had been cut short when he volunteered to stand in for a knife-throwing act; Hades also sent out for girls who could dance, and pipers who could play. None of these shadows gained the hint of a smile from mournful Persephone. Hades himself went on raids for bouquets of roses and chrysanthemums. What more could he do to make her feel at home?

If only she would eat. A relay of exquisite meals was sent along, all left untouched. Eventually Hades presented himself at the door with nothing but a single item of fruit: a pomegranate.

Persephone lay propped up in her bed. Pallid and unhappy as she was, her beauty still caused Hades to stumble in finding his words. In a gulped silence, while she maintained her downcast gaze, he passed the pomegranate from one palm to another.

'What I wanted you to know,' he said at last, 'is that when I took – took hold of you like that – it was my first roughness. It was, I promise, also my last.'

There was no response. He yearned to embrace her. He felt his gift of fruit to be feeble and poor. He laid it at the end of her bed, and retreated.

Some while after he was gone, Persephone stretched out, and took the pomegranate. She cradled it to her cheek. It was plain to look at. Its skin was tight and hard. Who would guess it had an inner cargo of such sweet and sparkling seeds?

Next day the juggler was recalled; and for the first time in the doleful regions of Hades, the glory of laughter was heard.

When Zeus finally made his way to the depths he was blowing his fingers and shivering extravagantly. But what he came across was warming enough. A king and a queen sat upon their thrones. They were in audience to their wispy subjects, conducting a session of assize. The king was stern in his demeanour, considered and grave while passing judgement. But the young queen was active too: giving her counsel, adding words of mitigation; easing the proceedings by her very presence. Clearly they worked in accord; discreetly, their fingers were entwined. For all that it was dim underground, Zeus saw his brother in a new light.

When the court was adjourned, Zeus paid his compliments to the couple, and explained the distress that had beset the world above.

'But am I right in thinking,' said Zeus to Persephone, 'that this state of wedlock does not entirely displease your majesty?'

The look exchanged between Hades and Persephone carried the unmistakable complicity of a couple ashamed to confess the pleasures they had discovered in each other. Yet Persephone admitted it: she missed her mother, her friends, fresh air and birdsong, more than she could say. Hades nodded. He was vaguely amazed, to find himself loved by this girl. And since he was loved, he begrudged her nothing. So it was, in the end, not difficult for Zeus to arrange a compromise. Let Persephone share herself. For half the year, she should stay with her husband, as his new-found, and ever-renewable, grace and solace. For the other half, Persephone was free to go once more among the deathless elements that had raised her.

Sensing the gist of this agreement, parts of the upper world suddenly erupted. A farmer digging ditches was one moment staring over his bleak and blighted terrain; the next thing he knew, he was flailing in lush thrusting sedges and cow parsley up to his eyes. On one mountain slope, two weary herdsmen fell asleep in a patch of barren scree – and woke up to find themselves embedded in clover, harebells and blueberry bush.

Demeter was appeased – although, as she knew, it was childhood's end. Each year she would welcome her Persephone with greenery and flowers, and bask in their togetherness through the months when all earthly growth matures. Then would come the time for Hades to be joined by his queen, and Demeter would lapse, always bruised by familiar loss. Her fruits dropped from branches like heavy tears; she gathered mists as a veil around her. At the mid-point of Persephone's retreat, it can seem to mortals that the quick sap of plant life is locked into a chill from which it can never escape. But it shall; as a matter of course.

# II

# HEROES IN THE MAKING

# HERAKLES

The girl moaned. It was a sound full of significance to those who heard. They bustled into action, rolling up their sleeves, fetching what would be needed: pitchers of hot water, fresh linen, blades and needles. Mother, grandmother, sisters, servants and aunts – all were assistants to this princess, Alkmene, busying about in her quarters at the royal court of Thebes. As for Alkmene – she hardly knew they were there. She was in a place that was only herself, disconnected from them all. Waves of pain and energy were rising there, beyond words to describe. So much life was on the move within her; Alkmene thought she must surely die.

She crawled, bent double. Breath whistled out of her: she was urged to suck in more. Squatting, she reached into a mist of tears and pain. It might have been a bedstead that she gripped, or else a bony shoulder: whatever it was, she braced herself against it, and she would have bitten it, too, had someone not slipped a wad of willowbark into her mouth. She clamped the pith. What now? What was all that yelling in her ears?

She grew aware of blurry movements, slippery forms. Then a strange version of peace descended. Voices were becoming distinct.

'My,' said one, 'there's a bruiser.'

'Bless us,' said another, 'he looks hungry already.'

'Well,' yet another was saying, 'we called on Hera: look at the gift she gave – did you ever see such a boy?'

'Call him Herakles,' said the first voice, decisively: '"Hera's Glory". As he is, and no mistake.'

Alkmene closed her eyes. *Hera*, she thought – *no, please, not Hera. Hera must know nothing of this.*

But it was too late. Hera, soother of the pangs of birth, was already there. The goddess had disguised herself as an old crone, and was mingling with the hubbub of women around the royal crib. She felt pleased: the mortals here were praising her favour at this remarkable delivery, a boy so immediately robust with promise and good looks. But as she slipped away from the scene, Hera caught the mutterings of an ancient palace nurse, tut-tutting as she went. 'I swear,' croaked the dame, 'no man fathered that!'

'Really?' ventured Hera from behind her shawl.

The old woman paused, and peered cautiously around: they were still in the royal precincts. 'All I'll say,' she confided, 'is that there's bodies of ours and bodies of theirs, and this is one of theirs.'

'Whose d'you mean?' hissed Hera.

'Hah!' said the nurse, hobbling away, and nodding skywards with a cackle. 'From up there, I shouldn't wonder.'

Hera did not need to launch an investigation. It was all too plausible. She had yet to forgive her husband for taking up with a mortal boyfriend – a giggling farmhand. Now, it seemed, he would humiliate her further, betraying her on earth as in heaven. How long before this Herakles – the so-called 'Glory of Hera' – was recognized as none other than some stray litter of Zeus?

Hera planned a quick revenge. That night, the palace of Thebes was breached by a snake. It flickered across the room where baby Herakles lay tucked up in a basket, close by his sleeping mother. The reptile arched over the cradle, poising to strike. A pudgy hand reached out, and tried its grip upon the glinting visitor. The snake lunged, spitting venom. But Herakles only chortled, and clutched harder. A set of small fat fingers closed and dug deep with a squeezing, unstoppable force. Then there was a distinct click. A backbone snapped. The snake slid broken to the floor.

Little Herakles had defeated his first monster.

Did Hera abandon her resentment at that? Of course not. But she held her anger in reserve. Let the infant prodigy prosper for a while. There was some fun to be had in testing him later; and, after all, the victim must know what life was like – if he was to be hurt hard by losing it.

So Herakles flourished through his youth. The question of parentage stayed obscure, since his mother Alkmene had a husband, who duly became king at Thebes, and by whom she bore two further sons. One was called Eurystheus. From the outset, Eurystheus never accepted Herakles. Growing up lanky and pale, Eurystheus loathed the hearty enthusiasm with which Herakles made every occasion a race, a challenge, a bout. The younger half-brother was Iolaus, who took a different view. No sooner could he walk than Iolaus followed Herakles, in a spirit of puppy-like devotion. When Herakles went to wrestle, it was Iolaus who carried along his flask of oil and rubbed his limbs; Iolaus, too, who brought the sharp-edged scraper that athletes use to shave off mud and sweat. Iolaus adored Herakles not so much because he was the invariable winner, but because, whatever was happening, to be close to Herakles was to know that fear was somewhere else. For his part, Herakles loved Iolaus as a boy who never refused a game – even if it was simply skimming stone discs across a pool.

While Eurystheus brooded indoors, plotting his chance for a kingdom of his own, young Iolaus learned how to handle a chariot. Soon he was skilful enough to drive Herakles to the plain of Olympia: a site where both Zeus and Hera had been honoured for as long as mortals could remember. At Olympia two rivers flowed through meadowlands where calves fattened on sweet grass and willow bushes hummed. Herakles and his sporting friends liked to meet here for their competitions: to see which of them could lift the biggest boulder, sprint quickest between the rivers, and so on. After one such feat of strength – Herakles not only raised a massive rock, but lobbed it clear over an olive tree – they heard an abrupt boom of thunder, and took it as a signal of applause from Zeus. So the lads decided to set up a special festival at Olympia, a celebration of physical effort that would please the gods. They laid out sandpits to wrestle in, and pegged targets for throwing. Herakles paced six hundred of his feet to mark the length of a stadium, set within sloping banks from which, eventually, onlookers might cheer runners and riders. Herakles decreed the prize: a crown of olive leaves to the fastest, the strongest, the one who boxed most fearlessly.

It was after one such Olympic gathering that Hera played her next deadly game with Herakles.

He was married now, with infants of his own; he was preparing to become, before very long, the ruler in the palace at Thebes where he himself had been born. That Herakles would make a fair and steadfast leader was widely expected; meanwhile there was no doubt that his appetite at least was fit for a king. To those who had joined with him at Olympia, Herakles offered a generous feast. He was last to leave the table – singing, and waving the thigh bone of an ox which he and his sparring partners had picked clean.

Murderous fury ensued. Possibly his wife greeted him with

36

words of reproach; probably his senses were adrift in wine. But only a heaven-sent madness could have pushed Herakles to swing that hefty bone so furiously within the walls sheltering his own family. One blow, and his partner's lifeblood was sprayed across the house. As for the children who awoke at her scream – their skulls were cracked open like eggs.

Amid the wreckage Herakles collapsed. He was still whimpering, and muttering to himself, when at first light he stumbled towards a remote marsh, carrying a length of rope. By the water's edge he located a good-sized stone, and knotted the rope around it. Then he fastened the rope about his own neck, and hoisted the weight. Now one great fling to clear the shallows . . .

But the goddess was not going to let him go so easily.

'What're you fishing for there?'

Herakles looked up. An emaciated, greybearded angler, poling his skiff through the reeds, was regarding him with mordant interest.

'Leave me be,' said Herakles.

The old man cocked his head. 'Fine chance I'd have, if I tried to stop such a foursquare brute as you.'

He paused, and punted a little closer. 'You know what they'll say?' said the fisherman, knowingly. 'They'll say you took the easy way out.'

'The easy way?' gasped Herakles.

'Of course. Now I don't know what you've done that brings you to this; but I do know what you're doing now, and I call it shirking. That's what they'll say. You shirked. You couldn't take the punishment.'

The sanctimonious intruder came closer still. 'I'll tell you something else,' he said, softly. 'It takes more than water to purify a man.'

Then he moved off, humming to himself. Herakles lowered

the stone, and for a while did nothing but examine the dark stains on his swollen hands. Slowly he untied the knot about his neck. He judged a direction by the glow of the rising sun. Then he set himself to walk towards Delphi: the shrine in the northerly mountains where the god Apollo issued forth advice. As Herakles did not begin to understand what strange violence had caused him to harm those whom he cherished, so he could not fathom by what means he could make amends. He was not a shirker; shirking was not his style. When hurt, he endured. If someone met a punch that dumped him in the sand, Herakles always whispered by his side: 'Be brave. Brave. Get up . . .' But here was something else. He had wrought destruction on the defenceless, in a rage that remained a mystery to him. Those victims would never get up; he could not bring them back. What on earth could he do – to express his remorse, to cleanse himself of the deed?

Apollo's oracle at Delphi was precise enough: *'Serve twelve times the King of Tiryns, to the best of your strength. Serve one year a Queen of Asia, to the least of your strength. Then your crimes will be discharged.'*

As with every Delphic counsel from Apollo, this message emerged as a strange goaty cackle through a fissure in the ground. The priests at the site listened carefully, inscribing the sounds; with due gravity they told him what the god decreed.

Herakles pondered the information.

'You're sure,' he said, at length, 'it was the King of Tiryns? It couldn't be any other king?'

The priests nodded. 'And a Queen of Asia,' added one of them. 'For one whole year.'

'Yes,' said Herakles. 'I heard that.' He drew a deep breath. 'Better report for duty, then.'

So he trudged towards Tiryns. There was little to cheer him

on the way except, with a quick rattle of hooves and wheels, the arrival of a loyal ally – Iolaus, who had ignored the many voices warning him that Herakles was mad and best avoided. 'Little brother,' said Herakles, sadly, 'what do you think of me now?'

'Enough,' said Iolaus. 'Get on board; and tell me where we're going.'

'To serve the King of Tiryns,' said Herakles.

'Tiryns?' queried the driver.

'Yes,' Herakles grimaced. 'To be purified in mud.'

News travels faster than a chariot. So the King of Tiryns was primed for the arrival of his novice servant. He twined his thin fingers and smiled. How satisfying: to be invested with the obligation to make a misery of Herakles. Dear, dear Herakles . . .

They did not come immediately face to face. Abasing himself, Herakles begged an audience with the king. The king nodded, with an equally extravagant show of condescension. Then the two sons of Alkmene regarded each other. It occurred to Herakles that the neck of Eurystheus resembled a young shoot of asparagus. It occurred to Eurystheus that Herakles quite lacked a neck.

'So what,' said Eurystheus, 'can you do for me?'

'Whatever,' said Herakles, 'is your wish: times twelve.'

Eurystheus sniggered. 'Is that what you sportsmen call a *dodekathlon*?'

'Of sorts,' agreed Herakles.

Eurystheus was not capricious. He had already conceived of ways in which his kingly power might be extended by having, at his disposal, what amounted to a highly effective one-man army. Only a few days previously, a delegation of farmers from the land of Nemea had petitioned his assistance in tracking down an animal that was plundering their livestock.

Rumours told of a tawny-coloured beast whose claws could bring down a bullock in moments; teams of trappers from all over the land had so far failed to catch it; already several distinguished hunters had lost their lives in the pursuit. As Eurystheus reasoned: either Herakles would fail – in which case, the next in line for the prestigious throne of Thebes was Eurystheus himself; or else Herakles would prevail over this monster – in which case it could be publicly presented as a daring initiative on the part of King Eurystheus.

'Let's start,' said Eurystheus, 'with a challenge I know you'll enjoy. It pits you against opposition in your own league, of your own kind one might say . . . '

Herakles listened to the commission without protest or questioning. He went to where Iolaus was waiting for him, outside the city gates.

'Which way?' asked faithful Iolaus.

'Sure you want to come?' asked Herakles. 'Actually it's nothing too impossible: a bit of hunting, that's all. We head up to Nemea.'

'Ah,' said Iolaus, 'I think I've heard about this.' Herakles began inspecting his bow, and testing the tips of his arrows. 'You can forget that,' said Iolaus. 'They've tried all sorts of missiles, and swords.'

True. The beast that was terrorizing Nemea was a huge lion, fearsome enough by itself, but a creature which Hera, foreseeing the challenge to Herakles, had also rendered invulnerable.

The two companions arrived in a valley that was eerily bereft of the many herdsmen and smallholders who had once prospered there. Herakles knocked at the doors of several farmsteads, hoping to get information about the lion: each lay in abandoned disarray. But soon enough there was fresh evidence of trouble. A huddle of milk-cows stood by a barn, lowing mournfully; in their midst were relics of horn, hoof and blood-sprayed hide. Iolaus stooped and picked up a felt hat, the sort worn by local peasants. He shivered. 'Still warm,' he whispered.

The trail of blood took them upwards to a cave, set behind brambles and fern. Herakles unsheathed a dagger.

'I told you, knives don't hurt this thing,' said Iolaus.

'I don't want any scratches,' said Herakles, slashing at the undergrowth.

In its recess, the lion was feasting and drowsy: but quickened when it heard this noisy approach. Iolaus froze where he was: some distance below, he saw the lion stiffen and crouch, with Herakles cheerfully swiping his way ahead.

For a few seconds – to Iolaus, it seemed beyond any reckoning of time – Herakles and the lion stared directly into each other's eyes. Deliberately, Herakles tossed his knife aside. Then the lion sprang: and in a thrashing bundle, Herakles and the lion rolled together into the thicket. There was a rapid turning and spitting and breaking of branches; finally, a concealed, compressed silence. It took all the courage that Iolaus could muster, to step gingerly towards that quietness. He could hear heavy panting in the undergrowth – but whose was it?

A voice gurgled up. 'Hey,' it called, 'this you should see.'

Iolaus burst forward. Deep in the thorns lay a large golden form. All that could be seen of Herakles was a pair of brawny arms, almost affectionately clamped around the neck of the warm but lifeless lion.

With a grunt Herakles shifted himself beneath. 'Dummy backward roll – double armlock. He fell for it.'

Iolaus made himself useful, pinching or sucking the thorns from his brother's punctured flesh. He found one sharp edge that could pierce the lion's skin: the lion's own claw. So it was that when Herakles returned to the court of Tiryns for his next challenge, he wore a new attire. Eurystheus was not the only one who went pale at this apparition: a man clad in the scalp of a lion. It was not so much a trophy as a costume that simply declared: Here comes the hero with a lion's heart.

Since many people also praised the wise command of Eurystheus, the king quickly assigned a similar task. This time, Herakles should tackle a monster called the Hydra, which lurked in a swamp in the territory of Lerna, not so far from Tiryns. Periodically there were sightings of the reptile, said to have a multitude of heads, each rich in poison; but folk tales could not agree whether it was five heads or five thousand. 'Perhaps,' mused Iolaus as he and Herakles travelled towards the desolate shore, 'the thing grows as many heads as it likes.' Iolaus was right: so long as lifeblood flowed from the Hydra's limbs, there was no limit to the generation of new parts. Hera had made sure of that.

'You'll let me use these, perhaps?' said Herakles, patting his beloved knotty club, and shaking his bow and quiver.

'I want you to use this, too,' said little Iolaus, rapping his own chest.

Their chariot reached the marshlands of Lerna: a bleak place lying below a foggy pall. 'Now where?' wondered Iolaus.

'That way,' pointed Herakles. Iolaus picked up the reins, adding as an afterthought: 'How d'you know?'

'Good question,' said Herakles. 'I don't. But something – or someone – is telling me so.'

Herakles was serving penance. In their separate ways, both Hera and Eurystheus were determined to see that he suffered fatally in the process. But Herakles, though he did not yet know it, had also gained an ally – a powerful ally: Athena no less, the divine daughter of Zeus. For reasons of her own, Athena had no cause to be fond of Hera. She knew why Hera had taken umbrage at the very existence of Herakles, but she failed to sympathize. Why should one stalwart mortal be hauled through misery because he happened to have his origins in some forgotten passion of her father Zeus?

Athena knew perfectly well where the Hydra of Lerna had its lair. The least she could do was give Herakles a gentle indication.

So Herakles and Iolaus were led to a dank range of reeds, bogs and osier beds. Such daylight as visited this place was draining away; their first job was to kindle a fire. Herakles dipped one of his arrowheads into pitch, and soon had the shaft in flames. He shot the brand towards a far-off clump of rushes. There was a hissing disturbance within, and a rumpus in the water. Then they caught sight of the Hydra: indignant, and probing around with more heads than could be counted – searching to spit venom at whatever had caused the fiery intrusion. Herakles picked up his club.

'I'm coming too,' said Iolaus, grasping a spear.

'No,' ordered Herakles; 'give cover.'

Herakles waded out to meet the advancing Hydra, and rapidly dealt well-aimed blows as various fanged heads spat towards him. Herakles hit hard and true: the heads that tried to bite him went flying. But no sooner had one head been detached than another, or two, sprouted in its place. The more Herakles swiped, the more he was beset.

Iolaus saw his chance. He grabbed a burning log from the fire they had made, and scurried forward to where Herakles, now sweating and desperate, seemed to be losing the battle. 'You strike,' urged Iolaus, 'I'll scorch.' And so they worked in unison. As Herakles clouted away one waving head, so Iolaus darted forward with his torch, and seared the wound with a sizzling poke. No new heads grew where the blood was staunched. The attackers ducked about, each guarding the other, until finally all that remained of the Hydra was a stump of congealed sores.

For much of the journey back to Tiryns the two men were mute with exhaustion. But before they reached the city, Iolaus put a question to Herakles.

'This being brave – is it something I can learn?'

'You did well out there,' murmured Herakles. 'Very well indeed.'

'Maybe,' said Iolaus. 'But you went first, as always. Is there a secret? I want to know.'

Herakles pondered. 'It's an act, isn't it? The power of make-believe. The odd thing is . . . promise you won't laugh . . . I used to get fired up by believing that my opponent was some maniac – yes, a maniac – coming after my wife and children. Now? Now – I've got nothing to defend. In that case – if you see what I mean – nothing to lose.'

Whatever Iolaus made of this advice, he was given little chance to try it. Back in Tiryns, Herakles obediently sought out his next assignment. Eurystheus gave instructions: they concerned the capture of a magical deer in the hills of Keryneia. But as Herakles made to go, Eurystheus called out to him: 'By the way. You seem to have forgotten something. These are your labours, are they not?'

Herakles nodded.

'Good,' smiled Eurystheus. 'Let's remember that, shall we? But in case you forget, let me advise you that your devoted provider of transport – our little brother Iolaus – has been detained, on the serious charge of aiding and abetting a known murderer. I have had no choice but to order his death.'

Herakles gazed at the grinning king. He said nothing, while his knuckles went white; then turned, bleakly, and left.

For several months the hero lived wild and spoke only to himself. He dwelt in tracts of forest never bitten by an axe.

His bed was a gathering of bracken. He ate what he could forage or snare. He studied spoors and tracks. Patiently, disconsolate, Herakles learned the habits of the animal he had been charged to catch.

One night she came down to the pool and he saw her from his hide. He had his bow pulled taut. It was a clear shot to the heart. But something stayed his arm: an instinct of respect. There was a being, ringed in moonlight, stooping to take water. She was not to be pierced like this. So Herakles lurked there for many more days and nights, stalking again, fashioning traps. At last he lured the hind, bound her legs, and carried her down from the tree-dense heights. Her rapid pulse thudded through his head. On his way back to Tiryns, he passed a rustic sanctuary to Artemis. The worshippers were astonished to see his load: it was a creature sacred to their goddess, glimpsed but never seen; it must not be harmed. 'I have not harmed it,' said Herakles, setting down the deer. A priestess undertook to hurry off and tell Eurystheus. 'Ask him what next,' Herakles called out.

What next was another beast: a boar, grossly oversized, that had been rampaging in the lands of the river Erymanthus. 'This time,' Eurystheus insisted, 'I want to see the spoils myself: understood?'

Herakles got the message. He followed the boar up to the snowline and pinned it down; trussed it up, and brought it into Tiryns. Court officials tried to block him as he strode through the palace. 'The king's in council,' they protested, 'he mustn't be disturbed!' But Herakles barged on, with the tusky hog on his shoulders twitching its slabs of muscle and blinking its dark little eyes. In his chamber, Eurystheus clutched at the arms of his throne, while his advisers scattered.

'As you requested, highness,' grunted Herakles, lowering his enormous load, and kneeling to unbind it.

'Did I?' panicked Eurystheus. Then, as the boar began to snort and run: 'How am I supposed to get out of here?'

'Use your legs, my lord,' said Herakles tersely, adding, under his breath: *'Those two streaks of piss hanging down from your waist.'*

Eurystheus dived into the nearest place of refuge: it was one of the huge clay storage jars that stood to collect the tithes and taxes he exacted from the people he ruled. Herakles let the boar run about and make its mark on the palace before he subdued it again. 'Lively little creature!' he remarked to Eurystheus, when finally the king crept out of his pot.

Humiliated, Eurystheus vowed further revenge. He would impose on Herakles ever more disagreeable tasks. So came the charge to assist a fellow petty ruler, called Augeus, whose territory included Herakles' beloved site of Olympia. Petty though he was, Augeus maintained the largest stock of cattle and horses anywhere in Greece. The challenge to Herakles was to relieve the exhausted stable hands there – lads dropping from the non-stop effort of sweeping muck out of the stalls. Herakles surveyed the scene a while, awed by the mountainous job. Then Athena came, and whispered in his ear. Herakles called for a spade. But instead of using it to shovel the steaming piles of dung, he began to dig a channel alongside the animals' byres. Working into the night, he took his trench across fields, until it connected with the local river. He heaped a dam across the current. Then he stood at ease. Water gushed into his conduit, and flowed copiously through the stables. It purged them soon enough: the world's first sewage drain.

Next Eurystheus despatched Herakles to Stymphalos, a stagnant lake. The stench of the place was so foul that it kept everyone away. But an island in the middle of this lake was the breeding place of a flock of steel-clawed waterbirds, increasingly relentless predators of sheep, cattle and – latterly

– humans too old or too young to defend themselves. Holding his breath, and with his bow drawn for shooting, Herakles waded into the fetid shallows of Stymphalos, hoping to pick off the winged oppressors one by one. It was no use: not a single creature flapped into sight. Then he found something pressed into his hand: a set of clackety bronze castanets. He gave them a shake, and their report sent up a first flush of birds. Another, more enthusiastic rattle, and the entire flock went squawking skywards. Now Herakles could step back, and fire his arrows to swift effect.

He did not collect them all. Some he picked up and took to a rocky outcrop, where a young woman sat admiring his markmanship. She wrinkled her delicate nose and turned away; Herakles halted and bowed. 'Sorry,' he said. 'I'll bury the lot of them: straightaway. But – thanks to you; again.'

Athena smiled. 'My hero. You can do it. On you go.'

Herakles went on. He went south, to the island of Crete, where he subdued a colossal rogue bull gone ragingly out of control. He went north, to the steppe-lands of Thrace, where he threw a harness around a quartet of man-eating mares kept by King Diomedes, and drove them back to Eurystheus as a docile chariot team. He went eastwards into Asia, to a region ruled by the female tribe of Amazons, and took from their queen, Hippolyta, the golden belt she wore as an emblem of her royal authority. He went westwards to Hesperia, where the sun dips away from the world: to broach the domain of a three-bodied monster called Geryon, and abscond with a herd of cattle. It was the work of many weeks, to get those cattle back to Tiryns; but no sooner had Herakles delivered them than Eurystheus sent the hero back in the same direction. This time it was towards the place that Eurystheus deemed 'the edge of the world', where the great Titan Atlas was holding up the heavens. Eurystheus had heard tales of three golden apples, called the Apples of the Hesperides, which only Atlas could reach. The challenge for Herakles was to obtain those wondrous fruits. So again Herakles trekked westwards, high up into the mountains of the land beyond Libya. He found Atlas amid the vapours of low cloud, standing sullenly under the burden that Zeus had long assigned to him. 'You want what?' grunted Atlas. 'Apples? If you want those, then you'll have to take this –,' he said, rolling his eyes to the weight that sat on the top of his spine. Herakles agreed. He was short of stature, but not of will. Piling cushions and pillows around his neck, he took the load. With a deep sigh, then a chuckle, Atlas wandered off. Suddenly, Herakles feared he might have been tricked. What if Atlas never came back? But the simple colossus only roistered around for a few hours, before he ran out of things to do. Meanwhile, though Herakles never knew it, Athena was standing by. She had the skies in the palm of her upraised hand. The suffering hero was not alone. His cause had become hers.

The golden apples duly appeared, and were duly consigned to the king who had wanted them. But for Eurystheus, they brought little delight. By now he was tired of this trial. Whatever he imposed upon his hated half-brother, it was not enough. Quite the opposite. With each and every more impossible task, Herakles only seemed to grow stronger, wiser and happier; yet – and no less irksome to Eurystheus – more flexible, more questioning, more open to doubt. What next for the indestructible lump? Hunched in his throne, the King of Tiryns gave a careless shrug. 'Final task. What else can it be – but the last monster of all?'

Herakles looked quizzical. Eurystheus began to giggle. 'Death, you lumbering fool. Go on. Descend and give it a fright. Then come back – as we're sure you will.' Eurystheus shook with laughter.

Herakles turned away, but paused at the door. 'A souvenir, master?'

'Ah yes, yes. Let me see . . . well – if Death has its own home, the premises are sure to be guarded. So – bring it up – whatever it is that keeps watch on that miserable realm.'

Death and Herakles had long since ceased to be strangers. So he accepted the test with a nod. As he left Eurystheus, however, the king issued one last petulant instruction: 'Since I exterminated your beloved little helpmate,' Eurystheus called out, 'I don't know quite how you're accomplishing all this. But for the last time, let me stipulate, again, that the task is yours. So you shall – I decree – go it alone.'

There are ways down to the Underworld for those who would seek them: cracks in the surface of the earth that are known to have swallowed stray goats and mortals made fools by curiosity. Herakles came to the edge of one such fissure – and was met there by a tall figure in resplendent robes, helmeted and holding a spear.

'Well, my stalwart,' said Athena, holding out her hand. 'Shall we proceed?'

Herakles sighed, and relayed to his ally the parting injunction of Eurystheus. The goddess nodded, and gave him a kiss; and Herakles pitched himself into the gloom.

He crashed on downwards, slithering along dark tunnels in an almost freefall chute of icy crystals, pumice and dust. Groggy and dazed, Herakles at last found his feet in a cavernous and clammy hollow, utterly quiet, and filled with a sour, unmoving air. But this profound interior was not entirely deprived of light. Some yellowish glow subsisted beyond, and Herakles began to stagger in its direction.

Was it some kind of gateway? Maybe. But before he got much closer, he became aware of a sentinel figure crouched there. Herakles halted, and strained his eyes. He heard a regular breath, backed by a ticking growl. Its hackles rising, a huge dog sniffed the stale surrounds. Herakles thought to himself: *Simple strategies are generally the best.* So he stooped to pick up a stone – a movement in itself often sufficient to make most hounds turn tail. But no eyes blinked as Herakles threw the stone, which pinged against a rocky door. The ratchet-growl from the creature turned to angry barking; then, with a leap, the enormous guardian flung itself forward. With his right hand, Herakles grabbed for its throat. Then a second set of jaws came slathering at him, and he blocked them with his left. Then the attack was tripled – and the hero had no defence. He felt hot doggy breath in his face, heard the rip of his flesh – and saw blood squirting away from his wrist where the beast had clamped its third set of teeth and torn through the sinews. He tried, as of old, to tell himself to be brave. But a black fog rolled over him, and he swooned to the ground.

When his senses returned, he seemed to be lying in a bower, exquisitely decked with swags of evergreens and dried flowers. Herakles smiled. So this was it: his awakening in the afterlife. In a moment, he thought, he would raise himself, and see if he could find his wife and children. And faithful Iolaus – Iolaus must be somewhere close by . . .

Then he became aware of voices. He gazed up to a pair of faces. One was very pale, caring and beautiful; the other older – hairy and forbidding, but not unkind. 'The hound was only doing his duty,' said the bearded one, sternly.

'Hush,' soothed the young woman. 'Whoever you are,' she said to Herakles, 'please, just try to move your fingers for me.'

His torn arm had been wrapped in a poultice of dried leaves. He flexed the fist, and found it functioned perfectly. He shook his head in disbelief. 'There,' said the girl. 'Good as new.'

Wine arrived, and meat, and plates of honeyed barley cakes. Soon Herakles was chomping happily, as Hades and Persephone explained how Cerberus, their three-headed black mastiff, had come loping to find them – once his cornered victim was down. 'You were lucky,' said Hades. 'He could have polished you off in a trice.'

'Oh no,' murmured Persephone, 'he's an old softy at heart. Just like his master' – and she bent down to stroke the huge animal, now slumped by her feet, its three tongues lolling out.

'Perhaps he knew that, strictly speaking, you are my nephew?' Hades wondered. 'Though I have so many, I suppose,' he sighed.

To the gentle Persephone, and gruffly muttering Hades, Herakles explained the reasons for his trespass. The rulers of the netherworld wanted to know more, much more, about the eleven previous adventures, and the spite that had devised them; and they respected, of course, the unlamenting manner in which Herakles bore his fate. As Hades said: 'This Eurystheus – he sounds a nasty piece of work. But whoever he is, he shall stand before us, in due time. Nothing will be hidden from us then.'

Hades was reluctant, but Persephone persuaded him. Yes, Herakles might indeed take Cerberus for a walk into the upper world. The huge beast must be kept firmly on the leash; but, they reassured the hero, he was very well trained, and would obey Herakles in everything.

The reaction of Eurystheus, when Herakles strolled into the palace hall with Cerberus at his side, can be imagined easily enough. Once more the king stared, screamed, and then plunged himself into the nearest storage pot. Herakles let the dog sniff around, before leading him back to the depths. Then he reported back to Tiryns.

The twelve punishing labours had consumed as many

years. Herakles still loomed as a bulky and stubborn presence. But his spark of boyishness was long gone. His eyes were pools of pain, sunk deep in knowledge of the world. He was too weary for recriminations; and Eurystheus, for his part, had little spirit left. The king had gained no glory – only ridicule, and public humiliation.

So it happened that Eurystheus put Herakles up for auction; as if he were any common slave.

And so Herakles was purchased by a passing queen.

She had shimmering skin and proud cheekbones. It was towards Lydia, on the coast of Asia, that she transported Herakles along with her retinue. Her name was Omphale; and once arrived at her palace, she called Herakles for a private audience.

He found her curled lazily upon a couch, nibbling pistachio nuts. Her wide-set eyes wandered over his sturdy but submissive form.

'At your service, madam,' said Herakles.

'Yes,' drawled Omphale. 'You are.'

'Have you enemies – monsters – to despatch?' enquired Herakles.

'No more than usual,' said Omphale. 'I mean – I just might, if I feel like it, let you go out and do your manly things. But haven't you proved that by now – your manliness?'

Herakles retraced his memory. The phrase of the oracle came back to him: *Serve one year a Queen of Asia to the least of your strength.* What on earth did that mean?

Omphale was still smiling, but her tone suddenly sharpened.

'Anyway you belong to me. You are my slave. You will do whatever I want. Is that understood?'

'Yes,' said Herakles.

'No. Say: Yes, most worshipful and exalted mistress,' demanded Omphale.

'Yes, most worshipful and exalted mistress.'

'That's better. From now on, your one aim in life is to obey my whims, and please me.'

On the couch, Omphale uncurled herself, and extended a slender ankle. 'Slave,' she snapped. 'Kiss and adore my toes.'

Herakles scratched his head; then dropped to his knees. Cradling the queen's foot in his hands, he pressed his lips here and there. Soon Omphale was purring, and making little involuntary jerks as the hero brushed the tip of his tongue reverently over her flesh. Faint wafts of salt musk reached him, but he dared not stop, nor lift his eyes. He heard the queen eventually sigh, however, click her fingers, and persons enter the room – her maidservants, to guess from their instant tittering.

'Look what we have here,' said Omphale. 'Our very own tame lion!'

She pushed her foot full into the face of Herakles, and sent him crashing backwards. He lay prone as the queen stood astride him there, her hands on her hips.

'Oh, but we shall tame him some more. Much more.'

She dropped herself onto his chest. Then she tugged at his beard. 'We can't have him bristling like this. For one thing,' she cooed, 'it tickles me. And for another' – she turned to the girls – 'don't we all like to keep ourselves smooth?'

The music of merriment scarcely ceased in Omphale's palace over the following week, as Herakles was transformed by the queen and her handmaidens. He was shorn of his bodily hair and the locks about his head were set into ringlets. He was assigned no tasks – but they taught him to walk in high-heeled sandals while holding a water jar on his head. His lion skin was bundled away – in its place, swathes of floating chiffon and silk. They pampered him with oils; they softened the calluses on his palms. Hard to say what amused them most in all these games, but probably it was the sight of the heavy-set hero perched upon a spinning stool, trying to draw skeins from a basket of fluff. He fumbled the work, and Omphale slapped him, in a flash of temper. 'You thought spinning was for spiders, I suppose?' she cried. 'But this is what we women do each and every day; as Athena ordained.'

'If Athena says so,' said Herakles, humbly, 'it must be right and good.' And he bent over to unpick his tangle of threads. Then Omphale felt a rush of tenderness for the emasculated man, and flung her arms around his neck.

'You dear, simple thing,' she said. Then she whispered into his ear: 'Don't you know what it is I really want from you?'

'Not really,' admitted Herakles.

A hand rummaged deep into the folds of his silken gown. 'Come along, big boy,' murmured the queen; and she led him away.

To Omphale of Lydia, in due time, a little Herakles was born – happily to patter through her courts.

Thereafter, the hero himself was freed. He had done what had to be done. He wandered back to Greece by many other lands. People in various places still recall the lion-shrouded man who once passed their way, and claim it was for them that once he swung his knotty club. The adventures of Herakles grew wherever he went. But a quiet life was all he sought, and no more exertions beyond raising altars to Athena and the other beneficent gods. Even Hera, by now, had become fond of him.

His end on earth was ghastly all the same.

He had married again: a girl by the name of Deianeira. During their courtship, the following incident had occurred.

Herakles was out hunting one day, and heard some cries of distress. He headed in the direction of the alarm, and came to the edge of a wide river. On the other side of the waters, he could see that a lecherous old centaur – a creature half-man, half-horse – had trotted beyond its usual habitat, and was blocking the path of a girl. Herakles would have intervened in any case, but he recognized the frightened form of Deianeira. Across the torrent, Herakles boomed a warning. The excited centaur, Nessos, took no heed. Herakles shouted again, and Nessos glanced up from his overtures of lust. Who was this noisy passer-by? Nessos continued trying to straddle Deianeira, clouting her down with his hooves. Seconds later, a whistling arrow struck home in the centaur's heart, and his forelegs buckled under him.

There was a pack on his back, and it slipped onto the ground. His breath catching short, the centaur saw his lifeblood seeping towards the pack. Then Nessos gasped out to Deianeira, 'My dear,' he said, 'forgive me; I did you wrong. Your splendour overcame me. Let me make amends. In that bag – the finest wool. Promise me – tease it out – make a shirt of it – then give it to your love, and I swear: he'll . . . he'll never be faithless, no never, not so long as he lives . . . '

Deianeira watched, horrified, as the creature fell dead into her lap, and rolled the whites of its eyes. She heard Herakles, across the river, calling out for her. She signalled that she was safe; then, thoughtfully, picked up the centaur's precious pack.

In due time, Deianeira became a wife, and did as wives did in those days – tended a loom, and spent many hours surrounded by baskets of thread. Herakles proved an attentive and kindly husband. (Once, he amazed Deianeira by not only repairing her loom, but briefly testing it too: anyone would think he had done it before . . . ) But during her hours alone, Deianeira was prone to fret. She was married to a man twice her age, with so much wisdom of the world; a man still vigorous, a man whom the years made more handsome and dignified – a man who commanded affection wherever he went. She held up the stuff that Nessos had given her. It was, undoubtedly, the finest wool; it would make a marvellous garment. In a few days' time, she knew, Herakles was due to go and preside over a seasonal ceremony to Artemis, a festival at which there would be dancing choruses of girls budding into puberty. Her husband should look magnificent in a new mantle. And if he were to be tempted by some adoring nymph – well, she did not see in what way a simple shirt could keep a man faithful, but it could serve (she told herself) as a token of her trust in him.

So she wove busily, and in time for her husband's departure she had fashioned a tunic of matchless quality, which Herakles held up with wonder and gratitude. 'What have I done to deserve this?' he asked. 'It's for the ceremony,' said Deianeira, '– and, of course, to remind you of me.'

Herakles set out for the distant sanctuary with the shirt wrapped safe among his ritual equipment. He journeyed, as usual, on foot, joining bands of pilgrims on the way. After several days of walking, a large and exuberant crowd gathered at the forest clearing where the goddess was to be honoured. But it was only after Herakles had been gone a day or two that Deianeira happened to confide, to her mother, about the special gift she had made. Deianeira's mother nodded approvingly. What was the material that made it so special? As Deianeira explained, her mother's face turned pale. 'No good ever came from Nessos!' she cried. 'Whatever have you done?'

In tearful panic, Deianeira called up teams of messengers, to catch up with Herakles and destroy the shirt. They rode hard, non-stop towards the sanctuary. But they were too late. As their horses tore into the precincts, Herakles was emerging from a recess, donning the bright new robe. A gasp went up from the assembled worshippers: at first, because the gown appeared so pure and white; then, because the same gown seemed to be erupting all over with little knots of fire. Delight turned to horror as Herakles realized what was happening. He swiped at the flames with his hand; but the garment bequeathed by Nessos only burned more intensely. Herakles dropped to the ground, rolling over and over in vain fury to smother the heat. By now the shirt was gathering flesh for fuel. Herakles screamed to the skies. Bystanders came forward with water to douse him, but the whirl of fire only spurted and jumped more eagerly. It did not peter out until it had reduced the great body of Herakles to a small nub of ash.

What happened next was unseen by mortal eyes. As if in a dream, the hero found himself treading on ground as cool and smooth as marble. Someone was holding his hand: it was Athena, guiding him through mist towards the solid forms of pillars and halls. Herakles gazed in wonder at his own form. His last sensations were of being engulfed by a thousand hot and angry waves. Now it seemed as though he were restored – not to the body that had been consumed, but to the shape he was in when at his prime, pitching rocks and blocking punches at Olympia.

Athena brought him before a throned figure – powerful, bearded, not unlike himself – who boomed a welcome.

'Herakles, my son: come and join us. You are to begin your time again – in a manner of speaking; for what, to us, is Time?'

The question was addressed to the others standing round: Apollo, Artemis, Hermes, Hestia and the rest. Some nodded, some laughed. Grimy Hephaistos scowled. Then Zeus gave one of his apologetic coughs. 'There is, however,' he continued, 'something we think you ought to do. Herakles, Glory of Hera, now to be born anew ... would you mind ...?'

Zeus turned to the ample-bosomed lady standing behind his throne. Hera stepped forward. A low chair was brought to her by one of the attendant Olympians. She sat herself down, and pulled her robes aside to reveal one firm, creamy-pink globe.

She patted her lap. As if entranced, Herakles stepped up and, as softly as he could manage, lowered himself onto Hera's knees. For a moment, the queen of motherhood looked entirely content as the hero nuzzled her teat. But she recoiled when he did as he was told – and sucked with full force. Docile as he was, Herakles had lost none of his formidable powers. With a shriek of alarm, Hera pushed her oversize baby away. What Herakles drew from Hera's breast sprayed out in a great jet across the heavens.

And there it stays, amid the stars. We call it the Milky Way.

# THESEUS

This story arises from the misdemeanours of two kings.

First: King Minos of Crete. The symbol of his royal power was the bull. In the palace of King Minos at Knossos that animal was more than just highly prized as a side of beef. It was a mascot, an idol, and a sporting prop. Anyone who could do a somersault over its horns immediately became an honoured courtier. Royal bulls had their own grooms, their own hairdressers. No royal event was complete without a bull, decked in ribbons and flowers. And because Minos was such a connoisseur of bovine form, Poseidon made him a gift. The sleekest and sturdiest and most brown-eyed bull imaginable was sent to Minos by the sea god. There was only one condition: that when Minos had enjoyed parading about with this magnificent specimen, it should be dedicated in sacrifice to its donor. But when that time came due, Minos made his mistake. He held the sacrifice; but he replaced the gift with a lesser steer from his stock. Poseidon was not fooled, and soon took his revenge. The sea god caused Pasiphae, the wife of Minos, to fall crazily in love with the bull he had given. She bore a child that was part-human and part-bull. The king adopted this unhappy creature, but kept it out of sight, below his own residence. It was both a pet and a terror to him. Minos preferred, however, to let legends of its monstrous ferocity spread. This was the hidden 'Minos-Bull', or Minotaur.

Now to the other delinquent royal, King Aegeus of Athens. Aegeus had a careless affair with one of his subjects – a woman whom he could never marry. When she became pregnant, he took her away to a remote place called Troezen, and settled her there to raise the child. Aegeus left two tokens of himself, under a boulder: a sword, and a pair of sandals. If a boy were born, and the boy grew strong enough to shift the boulder, then let that boy make his way to Athens and be acclaimed for who he was. Otherwise Aegeus wanted nothing to do with his accidental offspring.

So much – so far – for two fallible kings.

The boy of Troezen was raised as Theseus. In due time, for a boyish boast of strength, he moved the boulder. But young Theseus was given no inkling of greater importance to this feat. He wore the sandals, because they happened to fit him well; he carried the sword because it was keenly forged, something to wave and brandish with pride. Eventually, he did set out for Athens. But that was only because he was ambitious to be a hero. The main population of Troezen was four-legged: it was a place that offered little prospect of heroic glory. Theseus went to Athens determined that his destiny went beyond a lifetime of tending goats.

So: he entered Athens one morning – and he walked straight into the midst of a most promising local crisis.

It was a panic that had happened in Athens before; but that did not make it any easier to contain. It was caused by a lottery – a lottery with prizes that nobody wanted to win. What Theseus witnessed as he came into the marketplace was a scene of grim selection. Potters and donkey-drivers mingled with philosophers and scribes; any one of them might be called by the elders who stood on a platform, fussing around a set of enormous clay jars. Theseus arrived just at the moment when one of the elders had taken a potsherd from one of the jars, and hollered out a certain family name. The hollering of this name caused a hush of astonishment in the crowd. Then the elders went into earnest discussion, and soon everyone began to chatter and look around. A man near Theseus began, nervously, to laugh.

'Has someone got something?' Theseus asked.

'Only what he deserves,' muttered the man.

Theseus then learned what this clamour was. Every other year the Athenians were required to pay tribute to an over-lord: King Minos of Crete. Long ago, Minos had sent one of his sons to Athens, to enforce Cretan rule. That son had been murdered – a crime that was punished hard. Minos presented the Athenians with a dilemma. Either he instruct his army to destroy all the city and its surrounds. Or else the city send him a selection of its own sons and daughters. Seven of each: striplings, to do with as he pleased.

'And what happens to them, over in Crete?' asked Theseus.

'God knows,' shrugged his informer. 'There're tales of a monster that Minos keeps, and some doomed place under-ground where people get utterly lost. All we know for sure is – our youngsters never come back.'

The buzz in the market, and the fussing up on the platform, had not abated.

'So what's happened, just now? What was the joke?' pressed Theseus.

The Athenian grunted. 'We're all in those urns. Anyone who lives here can be called on to give a child. But that name you heard wasn't just anyone's. It was our noble King Aegeus'.'

Theseus was a lad from the stony slopes. He knew nothing of Aegeus. Neither, back in quiet Troezen, were shudders caused by the fearsome repute of this Cretan King Minos.

Theseus was simply aware of his own ambition, which – after all – he had come into Athens to try.

' . . . and where is our great Aegeus now, eh?' the Athenian was saying.

But Theseus was not listening. The would-be hero was pushing forward to the platform where the city greybeards were still furiously quibbling among themselves, and seeking to impose order on the besieging crowd. He jumped up onto the platform.

'Here,' he said. 'Put my name down.'

This had a calming effect. At least it was a request that contradicted all the other protesters.

'Oh,' said one of the elders, suspiciously. 'And what might your name be?'

'Theseus.'

'Theseus who?'

'Theseus it is.'

The elders were nonplussed. Never, in the miserable history of this occasion, had anyone *volunteered* to go to Crete. One of them, though, began to grumble about protocol, and the problem of summoning the royal offspring of Aegeus.

'Forget it,' said Theseus. 'I'll find the others. I'll have them by nightfall.'

'All of them? And the girls?' demanded the elders.

'Leave it to me.'

Theseus had come as a stranger to Athens. He was young, handsome and unashamedly self-assured. What he was offering to do was something that would have been thought of as mad. And yet . . .

And yet boldness can be contagious. It breeds. One individual shows it, and others wish to be counted, too. The spirit distributes itself.

So Theseus did not lack for recruits. Throughout the day followers presented themselves. They came to him even as he busied around in the smiths' quarters of the city, assembling varied weaponry. By dusk Theseus was able to lead a band of young Athenians down to the harbour, where a ship stood ready to be boarded for Crete. As by custom, the sails of the ship were black, a mark of the city's despair. But to the dockside throngs Theseus and his entourage presented a jaunty gang. The elders peered curiously at the seven girls there. All long-haired, and wearing voluminous dresses, these were surely the most ungainly maidens the city had ever despatched to Minos; and a scribe, responsible for logging the names of those departing, raised his eyebrows when Theseus rattled them off: *'Rosy Lips?' 'Ox-Eyes?'* But the official was thankful that the victims of Minos were departing in such a docile and easy state.

A grandiose group made its way to the point of embarkation. It was King Aegeus, with his wife, his counsellors and a retinue of offspring. Theseus and his band lined up to be saluted by the king. Old Aegeus passed along, sadly nodding to each of them; he hardly dared look any in the eye. When he came to Theseus, he paused. One of his aides whispered in his ear.

'So,' said Aegeus, raising his gaze to Theseus. 'You are the boy who stepped in for the king.'

His eyes travelled over the hero's steady face and resolute figure; down to the ground where he stood. He spoke again, in a creaky voice. 'Young man . . . would you, please, show me your sword . . .?'

Theseus drew his blade from its scabbard. Aegeus rocked his head; his eyes glazed with tears, and he clasped the son he had recognized.

'Come back,' said Aegeus, at length. 'I pray you come back.'

'I shall. We all shall,' said Theseus. He was puzzled by the commotion in the old man before him.

They began to board the boat.

'We will be looking out,' cried Aegeus eagerly, as Theseus busied his crew. 'When you return, hoist up white sails – let us know you have prevailed . . . '

'We will!' shouted Theseus.

Tall, strong, easy, decisive: Theseus commanded naturally; and to hold himself unnerved by nothing was, in this young captain, a point of pride. But the landing in Crete shook even Theseus, though his companions were too wide-eyed to have noticed it, as they stepped off their trim craft. A hostile mob was already waiting on the quayside, with jeers about the unlikelihood of a return journey and malevolent offers to buy or scrap the boat. The Athenians were immediately harried by guardsmen along to the palace of Minos. They went under towered gateways, and fortress walls of giant stones; then along corridors that swallowed their footsteps, deeper and deeper into an echoing enclosure of ramps, niches, temples and storerooms. They saw wizened secretaries, scratching marks and tallies upon plaque after plaque; they glimpsed courtyards bright with painted walls, and flashes of lapis lazuli; they passed by a stained and reeking altar, above which towered the stern effigy of a woman flourishing a bunch of snakes in each of her fists.

And everywhere, everywhere, motifs of bulls; old skulls and horns of bulls; and the sign of the double-edged axe.

Finally they reached a set of colossal cedarwood doors. The head guard spoke.

'You – beast-fodder. Down on your hands and knees. When I open the door, you crawl forward. You don't look up till I tell you. You don't say a word till the king bids you. Understand?'

The Athenians looked to Theseus. 'Follow me,' said Theseus.

The doors swung open. There was a pillared hall, filled with finely dressed people; and there, set apart on a solid earthenware throne, was the hulking figure of King Minos himself.

Two girls stood either side of the throne. One was tall and wan, dressed demurely in white, like a priestess. The other one was younger, flashing with gold and jewels.

For a while the king said nothing, merely sending a quizzical look to the head guard. Theseus stood quite upright at the front of his group. He looked direct and cheerfully at Minos.

Minos coughed aloud. 'Our guests from Athens! A smooth crossing, I hope?'

Theseus maintained his fearless smile.

'You must be hungry,' continued Minos, with mock solicitude. 'Well, well. We'll be feeding you – feeding you terrifically, eh?' Minos turned to the assembly. A tinkle of conspicuous tittering quickened around the hall.

Then Minos examined one of the Athenians standing close to Theseus – a stout lass, it seemed, whose face was quite concealed beneath a mass of flaxen hair. 'By thunder,' he said. 'What do they call you?'

'Goldilocks,' intervened Theseus, briskly. He was still grinning. 'And what do they call you, Minos?' he went on, raising his voice. 'What are the whispers at the edges of your realm? How do they hail you, down in the rat holes of this great palace of yours? Slavemaker? Axemaniac? Taxgrabber, Bloodguzzler?'

His words clattered among the columns. Minos gaped. Theseus looked around now; his eyes rested upon the tall girl in white standing beside the throne, whose pale features seemed frozen by his recklessness.

'Is this how Minos rules – the useless pursuit of spite, year after year, into innocent homes?'

Guards closed around Theseus.

Minos was choking. 'Get out – you – you –'

'Theseus it is!' called Theseus. 'You won't forget!'

As he was dragged away, the hero glanced back at the pale girl. Her cheeks had gone fiery bright.

Eros had kindled again.

That evening the Athenians were each put in a cell, with sentries posted. Theseus was half-expecting the tap that came at his door in the deep of the night.

His cubicle was suddenly invaded with sweetness; another's lips closed upon his. 'Theseus,' she whispered.

'Brave girl,' murmured Theseus.

'Ariadne it is. A daughter of the man who's sending you to your death.'

'So he thinks.'

Ariadne sighed in the dark. How could she begin to relate the whole unhappy history of this palace? There were so many twists to describe. How her father Minos had been born from the abduction of an Asian princess called Europa – by Zeus, who had surged off with Europa to Crete, in the form of a strong white bull. How Minos had employed the inventive maestro Daedalus to make a writhing maze for the Minotaur, and how Daedalus himself had become lost in the puzzle he created ... Then, how clever Daedalus had escaped by devising wings for himself and his son Icarus, who, once aloft, had flown too close to the sun, so close that the wax that fixed his wings had bubbled up, and the boy dropped headlong into the sea. Everything seemed dark and crooked here; nothing ever straight.

Eventually Ariadne spoke. 'This – this thing you've heard about. They keep him – it – deep down below the room where

66

you were received. Theseus – it's a hateful, evil place. Utterly shut off from the sun. Tunnels that run and return and take you nowhere. An endless place; we call it the Labyrinth. You're trapped down there with – that beast.'

'Thanks,' said Theseus. 'Is that what you came to tell me?'

Fingernails punctured his back. Then Ariadne released him, and reached for a bag. 'Here,' she said. 'I brought these.'

She held out, first, a circular object, which, as she presented it, began to glow as if it were a ring of moonshine. Theseus took it, wonderingly. It was brittle, and warm to the touch.

'A crown of light. From the pits of the sea.'

Ariadne brought out something else. 'That's special,' she said. 'Whereas this – well, to be honest, any woman could have given you one of these.'

Theseus picked it up with equal wonder. Ariadne laughed. 'It's called a clew. No magic. Just a stick of wound-up thread. I said there was no way out,' she went on. 'There isn't. But there is a way in. Find your way back from there.'

Theseus gazed at Ariadne in the glimmer of the coral-circle: dark-eyed, serious, pallid as before. 'Why are you doing this for me?'

She turned away from him. Could this man be as dense as he was brave?

'Just promise,' she said, at last, 'just promise me one thing: if, somehow, you come out of the Labyrinth. Kick down the palace doors and take me away from here.'

'All right,' said Theseus, effortlessly. 'I will.'

'Tomorrow,' Ariadne continued, 'there'll be a ceremony. Speeches, incense, incantations. You'll all be let down into the Labyrinth. It's where they feed my – the thing. Fix the thread right there. I'll come at first light. There must be some way of getting out. If you're – if you've . . . '

She kissed him hard; and flung herself away.

Next morning it all happened as Ariadne had forecast.

In the throne room an altar had been raised, crowned by a knot of flames. Myrtle branches filled the hall with aromatic smoke.

King Minos bustled around, in priestly garb; other robed figures sang and drank from bulls' horns. Still others played rattles and drums.

In front of the king's chair, several henchmen lifted up a massive bronze grille. One craned his neck down the well-shaft below. He shrugged, and slung down a rope ladder. The chanting and drumming soared.

The guards were there to prod the Athenians forward; but Theseus went down without goading.

The ladder dropped him into a damp, cool gloom. He sniffed the air. It carried a faint reek – of dung, perhaps, or stale warm straw. Theseus fingered the coarse-carved wall around him; took a bronze pin from his garments, and tapped it into the wall with his sandal heel.

One by one his company came swinging down the ladder. There were pitiless guffaws high above; the grille clanged shut.

A few faint squares of light arrived at this depth. Theseus regarded his troops.

'Show us your thighs then, Goldilocks.'

The seven maidens shook off their tresses and tore the stuffing from their chests. Pulling aside their skirts, they revealed an arsenal of daggers and short-handled spears, all strapped to their legs. Theseus distributed them, and then indicated the yarn of the clew now tied to the nail he had fixed.

'Whatever you do – hold on to this.'

Several passages converged where they stood. Which one to take? Theseus had no more knowledge than any of the shivering lads. But, as ever, he brushed doubt aside, and opted by instinct for one of the ways, letting the spindle unwind to those who came in tow.

Almost immediately this passage made a sharp turn, and he was sealed in darkness. Behind him, the next boy stumbled and cursed. Theseus fetched Ariadne's coral-wand from his tunic and held it aloft. Its phosphorescence made a gloaming for some paces ahead. So onward he went. The turns were irregular, they came abruptly: at each angle Theseus paused and trained his nose. That rankness he had smelled when he first fell into the Labyrinth – it must be the scent of the beast, and he felt it was getting stronger. But the silence beyond was powerful too. He could only guess when the Minotaur might be found, and where to station his young companions. They, at least, should stay within calling distance of one another.

Forward, turn, stop. Back, turn; forward again.

Soon his nearest follower was left far behind.

The lack of help close by did not trouble him – so much as the rate of unravelling thread. That was the mystery of the maze: the sense, as in some dream, of having moved nowhere at all – and yet the thread had almost run out.

He made another turn. Then he halted. The trail of odour had become a stench. Theseus lowered his torch, and edged along the wall. Another turn.

And there it was. Or at least, he sensed it there: a rasp of breath, from some hot bulk, rising and falling. Theseus groped for the quiver of darts he had by his belt. He cut the last length of string, looping it to his left wrist. From the sweat and heaviness that hung about, he gauged that the Minotaur lay perhaps ten paces off. He pulled a long breath of his own, and felt for Ariadne's garland-beam. He tossed it towards the beast.

What formed in the shade was massive, but still. It was curled against a hollow in the rock, a bed strewn around with debris – straw, bones, palm fronds, relics of fruit. A black-furred dome of nape and shoulders shifted there.

Theseus spoke. 'Bull of Minos. Theseus it is. Theseus who sends you off.'

He pitched one of his darts vehemently towards the black-furred dome. The Minotaur jerked, and slewed around. Now Theseus could see two thick legs, joined to a huge torso; upon which was built the swollen, full-horned head of a bull.

The creature reached and scratched about its pelt, as if mildly stung by the bronze spike so solidly lodged. Stubby fingers plucked the missile out, where blood was bubbling forth. Theseus was briefly mesmerized. To see the Minotaur examine the spear – turn it over in its hands, with a human deftness – both horrified the hero, and yet brought forth a flicker of affinity. Was this a monster – or merely some rejected cross between man and animal? But Theseus had a second lance already in his grasp, and he loosed it fast, striking the Minotaur's forequarters; then another, aimed for the brow, which merely glanced off its horn-hard target. Now the Minotaur was erect, swaying, and lowering to charge.

'See the light!' hissed Theseus. 'Take it!'

The Minotaur swung its gaze to where Ariadne's gift lay warm in the dust; was curious, and stooped to reach. Theseus snatched forward, with a dagger this time, and drove it deep between the shoulder blades; the beast tossed its horns with a bellow of rage, and Theseus was sent spinning away. But he had hold of the thread still. He scrambled to his feet and tugged for the twine as he ran, crashing from side to side along the passageways. He heard the Minotaur heaving and hissing behind. Theseus shouted as he scuttled in retreat, partly to taunt his pursuer, partly to alert the others. One returned a shout, then another. In the close blackness the beast pitched among them, and collided with knives all around. There were shrieks, grunts, rollings to the ground.

And then quiet: apart from panting all around, and the groans of those whom the horns and fists had caught.

Each Athenian, now, wore a coat of blood. But each still had his life-breath – unlike the beast slumped amid them. Theseus felt for its forelocks, and stroked them with some affection. Nevertheless, he explored with a blade, and sawed the head away.

Ariadne's yarn took them back to where they had entered the Labyrinth; and there, at dawn, a voice called down to them, and a knotted rope came jerking down. The white-cheeked Ariadne stifled one scream, as Theseus appeared; then another, when she glimpsed what he was hauling up.

'Don't look,' said Theseus, planting the Minotaur's head square on the high-backed throne of Minos.

'He was my half-brother,' she sobbed.

Without any further word, Ariadne led them out of the palace and down to the quay, where the black-sailed ship was still anchored. They lost no time in getting away.

King Minos never gave chase – even though he controlled the seas all around. Once he had lost a son. Now a daughter, too, had been taken from him. And the head of a creature that bore his name lay beset by flies in a hardening puddle of blood.

Minos was too crazed to care. Theseus, in any case, took his ship on a zig-zag course; revelling in the company of all on board – except Ariadne.

The truth was that he had courage enough for everything but this passion. He felt the lurchings of her heart when she held tight to him, but it was a power that he could not match.

One night, when they had camped on a beach on the island of Naxos, Theseus left Ariadne as she slept, and stole away with his friends.

It was the god Dionysos who later found and comforted her, weeping herself to death by the shore.

On another island, flowery little Delos, Theseus stopped to give thanks to Apollo. He devised an erratic stomping dance there, called 'The Crane', because of its strange high-stepping moves. It was a mimicry of the maze. Forward, back, halt. Twist, stamp, stop. In, out, along, along; turn about, and strike. Forward, back, halt . . .

Heady with triumph, they made for Athens. Vaguely Theseus recalled his pledge to Aegeus, to change black sails for white if he should return. But what did it matter? Everyone would be the more delighted when they stepped off the boat. He never imagined that the old king would be scanning the horizon hour upon hour, hardly daring to hope; and that when the black sails came into view, Aegeus would stagger with anguish and guilt.

Heartbroken, the king threw himself into the sea that still bears his name – the Aegean.

Theseus was welcomed on a tide of popular gratitude; he was given the kingship too. Under his guidance, Athens was unified with its hinterland, and flourished. Theseus had walked into a shambles: he left it a city, strengthened by his own shrewd alliances of marriage – first with Hippolyta, queen of the tribe of warrior-women called the Amazons; then with a certain Phaedra, whose name means 'the Bright One'.

Phaedra liked to wear jewels and gold.

She was the only remaining child of a faded king. That king was a dishevelled figure who wandered, broken by grief, about the crumbling structures of his bull-proud palace at Knossos.

# PERSEUS

There was once a girl of very delicate beauty called Danae.

Her father Akrisios guarded her closely, and not only because he was protective of his daughter's loveliness. He had once been given a prophecy that the cause of his death would be his own grandchild. So he had Danae kept inside a bronze-walled chamber, secluded from all male company.

But what barrier could withstand the pressing desire of Zeus? As Danae's beauty was not secret from his eyes, so her body was not sheltered from his lust. The booming god simply passed through the cell in a shower of molten gold – and was all over her as he pleased.

With the help of her nurse, Danae tried to hide the result of this strange invasion. She pretended she was ill, she wore loose clothes; eventually, she managed to bear the baby without her father knowing it was due. But the little boy came with the same capacity as all mortal infants: to raise a noise out of all proportion to his size. Danae's predicament was out. Akrisios furiously demanded explanations. She could only sob that no man had been with her: only a warm and wonderful flood of gold – that had descended in waves and then flowed away as mysteriously as it came.

'A flood of gold?' Akrisios shouted. 'Is that what they call it now?' But he could get nothing but this story from Danae. He ordered his carpenters to make a large wooden chest. Into this chest he put Danae and her son, whom she had called Perseus, 'Destroyer', and had it loaded onto a boat. When the boat was well out at sea, he peered into the chest and repeated his demand that Danae tell the truth. All Danae could say, again, was that one night she had been visited by a surging, irresistible passion: warm and glowing – if not gold, then something like a god.

'Enough,' said Akrisios, pulling a lid over the chest, and grimly hammering it down. 'If it was a god – then let him take care of you now.'

With that, he heaved the chest overboard, and turned his ship away without waiting to see if it floated or sank.

The wooden prison stayed adrift, aimless in the waves. But floating seemed a thin mercy to the mother inside, as she crooned to the child at her breast. Sick, sleepless, without food or drink, must she wait till the last marrow in her bones was sucked dry? When after several days some fishermen off the island of Seriphos hauled in the chest and prised it open, they found a woman unconscious and close to death, with a weakly nuzzling baby still clung under her hunched form. The fishermen carried the pathetic pair to the island's ruler, Dictys, who immediately took care of them as if they were his own.

Years passed, and Perseus grew into a stalwart youth; while Danae's serene beauty was not only restored but deepened with age. Naturally enough, she attracted hopeful husbands. The most persistent of these was Polydektes, the brother of King Dictys. Polydektes had wealth behind him, and harboured no doubts about his own suave charm and immense social importance. After considerable efforts, he began to think that he was well on the way to winning Danae – if only she came without that insolent boy.

Between Polydektes and Perseus there was an instant, fierce and mutual dislike. At first Polydektes tried to ingratiate himself with presents for the child. But he became ever more painfully aware that young Perseus regarded him as not only an unwelcome intruder but also a pompous fool. Polydektes made sure that Perseus was not around when eventually he asked Danae to be his wife. When Perseus heard of the plan, however, he confronted his mother with disbelief and indignation.

'Mama,' he cried. 'You can't possibly marry that man.'

'And why not, my love?'

'Why not?' Perseus exclaimed. 'Why, why at all? He smells of onions. His face is always shiny and red – and he puffs when he has to move. He gave me a flute – a *flute* – when I wanted a knife. And–'

'And he's very kind to me,' said Danae, 'and would be to you, if you let him. His brother saved us both. You know that.'

Perseus shook his head. 'But – he can't even run!'

Danae laughed. 'Bless you, I don't want a man who can run. I want one who stays – someone solid.'

Perseus turned away – before his mother saw the tears boiling in his eyes. 'Huh!' he muttered. 'He's solid all right.'

Perseus did nothing to endear himself to his portly prospective stepfather. As for Polydektes, once he had gained Danae's formal acceptance of marriage, he allowed himself to express more often his hostility towards Perseus. It came to a head as preparations for the wedding were under way.

In those parts it was the custom for every male guest at a wedding to pledge a gift for the bridal pair. Something four-legged was the conventional offering; usually, a horse. Before a gathering of his cronies, Polydektes loudly asked Perseus what his gift would be.

'A Thracian steed? An Arabian mare?' Polydektes jibed.

Sulkily, Perseus said nothing.

'Sorry. I forgot,' Polydektes went on. 'Only the men are obliged to make gifts. I suppose we must count you a boy – the way you behave.'

'I'm more of a man than you'll ever be,' retorted Perseus hotly.

'Oh are you!' said Polydektes. 'Then what's it to be?'

Perseus thought about this. 'Something truly suited to you,' he announced. 'How about – the Gorgon's head?'

At this, everyone burst out laughing – except Polydektes, who stared hard at Perseus, and said, with quiet menace: 'Is that a promise, young man?'

Perseus nodded.

'Then you had better keep it,' said Polydektes. 'If not – your mother is entirely mine; and you shall never see her again.'

It was the divine Hermes who came across Perseus hours later, alone and shaking with remorse. Always on the move, Hermes wandered past in the guise of an old vagrant, a felt bonnet slanted on his head. Hermes was the god of solving problems: naturally he was curious and inclined to help this moping youth.

'Trouble with girls?' Hermes asked Perseus.

Perseus shook his head. He explained the predicament he had created for himself by vowing to fetch the Gorgon's head. 'I don't even know where to find the beast,' he sighed.

'Ah,' said Hermes. 'The Gorgon. There are three of them, actually. They lurk in darklands of the west, I've heard. The one you want is called Medusa. Well – when is the wedding?'

'The day after tomorrow.'

'Then you'll need to move quickly,' said Hermes.

'Tell me something I don't know,' groaned Perseus.

'All right,' said Hermes. 'I'll tell you that you need some of these.'

The god pulled up his vagabond's trousers, to reveal a pair of neatly winged sandals. As Perseus stooped to take a closer look at them, Hermes suddenly rose aloft and darted away. He was a speck in the sky; then Perseus lost sight of him. But no sooner had the god disappeared than he swooped back and resumed his stance, without so much as catching his breath. Perseus was agog.

'So,' he said to Perseus. 'Want them?'

Perseus nodded.

'They're yours,' said Hermes, kicking off the sandals. 'Right. I've told you where Medusa's to be found – roughly. What d'you know about her?'

'Not much,' admitted Perseus. 'What all children are told. That if you take one eyeful of her horrid face, she turns you into stone.'

'That *is* the main thing to know,' said Hermes cheerfully. 'Medusa has looks to kill. Although,' he mused, 'how does anyone know? If they never live to describe the Gorgon's gaze? That's her power, I suppose.'

'What is?' asked Perseus.

'The unknown. Prime source of mortal fear. Don't you fear fear, young man?' demanded Hermes.

'Not sure what you mean,' Perseus replied.

'Lucky you,' said Hermes. 'Perhaps you'll stay that way. Now – I've a couple more things to help you on your mission.'

Hermes reached into his cloak and produced a slightly curved round shield, unadorned, with a simple leathern handle.

'This comes from Athena.'

Perseus took it. The metal was brightly silvered, but lightweight.

'I hear what you're thinking,' Hermes went on. 'It's small, even girlish. What do you expect me to lug around? But there's a message from the goddess: Used wisely, this will deflect the heaviest of blows – or words to that effect.'

Then he handed to Perseus a weapon. This, too, was easy to carry. Yet within the sleek black sheath was a long blade of flashing finesse and keen efficiency. 'You'll agree that's quite a knife,' said Hermes.

'I'll say!' said Perseus, turning it over with awesome gratitude. 'This is just what I've been wanting –'

He looked up. There was much more he wanted to ask. But his ragged benefactor had vanished.

Perseus was not distressed. He could not wait to try his newly acquired power of aviation. He had only to think where he wanted to be, and the feathered sandals took him there, fast as thought. He went flying up into pure heights cushioned by clouds. He looped, he dived, he soared; he loved the whistling past his ears. He spent the afternoon teasing songbirds and buzzards alike. Once he was alarmed when a great tawny eagle came towards him, thrashing its wings with talons outstretched. But when Perseus pulled out his knife, the eagle veered away. Then, as the sun began to decline, Perseus settled into a westerly windstream, and let himself glide along, just below the scatters of cloud.

By and by he neared something very solid. It was the rugged Atlas, still holding up the skies. Or so poor Atlas thought. As Perseus could clearly see, it was a futile task. The skies would stay up perfectly well without such support. Perseus hovered by the Titan's surly face, and gave him this happy news.

Atlas glared at Perseus. The brief respite from his burden brought by the visit from Herakles had left him vaguely aware that there was some mockery about his perpetual show of strength. 'Another midget trying to prove himself?' he growled. 'Get on. Leave me be.'

'I only want your help. Tell me where the Gorgons are. From where you stand you must know.'

'Might do,' muttered Atlas. 'But wouldn't tell an insect like you.'

'Thanks,' said Perseus, flying on. 'I'll remember that.'

Perseus knew the ghastly sisters could not be far away. As he circled high over the lands below, he began to think through his strategy of attack. He must catch Medusa by surprise, perhaps while she was sleeping. She was the only Gorgon who could be killed; but she was also the only Gorgon whose gaze absolutely should not be met. Perseus held up the dainty shield that Athena had provided for him, and sighed. What safety could this possibly offer against three furious monsters? Suddenly his own features beamed from its glimmering rim. Of course – that was its pretty trick. He could look on Medusa as long as he liked – so long as the shield took her stare.

Eventually he spied a tract of the earth's surface that was clearly devoid of mortal habitation. As he made cautious descent, forms took shape on the ground. There was an elephant, head lowered to charge; over there, a crouching lioness. Further on, he saw a party of hunters, advancing with their spears.

But all were utterly immobilized – installed around this desolate place like statues.

Perseus dropped lower, in amongst a clump of gloomy elms. Something squeaked and startled past his face. He recoiled, and glared into the branches. Then he saw that the trees had a strange fruit festooned from them: odd bundles of feathers and twig; the flaky skins of strung-up reptiles; a line of yellow gut threaded with teeth and bits of bone.

The objects rattled in a shudder of the evening breeze – the same breeze that sent a chill through his own frame. Another screeching rodent brushed his cheek, and Perseus swiped at the thing. But his hand knocked an object hanging from a bough, causing it to spin crazily.

It was a makeshift effigy of bark and moss, with stark arms and splayed legs. At the end of the legs were two carefully fashioned slippers, each finished at the heel with a distinct feathery wing. The face was a gurning caricature of pain. Where the eyes should be – two needles had been thrust.

For some moments Perseus was intrigued by the bobbing doll. Then, without knowing what he was doing, he clutched for the upper air, and struck high again. He did not come down again until he was at the edge of the morose landscape. There he found himself by a shelter of rock. The first thing he heard was a clattering noise. It came from his own jaws. His mouth went dry. He realized that his entire body was shaking. He tried to move. But all firmness had deserted his knees. He tried again. This time, something flicked in the pit of his stomach, and a jet of tanging urine squirted down his legs.

Perseus curled up, and began to sob. Perhaps he cried himself asleep. But when he peeped out from the shivering bundle he had made of himself, there was a woman standing there.

'*Mama?*' gulped Perseus. But even as he spoke, he knew it could not be.

'Not her,' said Athena, softly.

Perseus looked up. The goddess stood very tall before him, robed from her shoulders to her toes, holding a long javelin, with a huge crested helmet upon her head.

'No cause for shame,' she said. 'You had never before set foot away from that little island – and now we launch you over continents. You've spent a boyhood whittling sticks. What training is that – to succeed where so many skilled trackers and dauntless spearmen have met their end?'

Perseus was mystified none the less. 'But why?' he implored Athena. 'Why did I fly away like that, and shake, and – and disgrace myself?'

'Because,' said Athena, 'you came within the shadow of the Gorgons' lair: which is the breeding-ground of fear.'

Perseus remembered the question put to him only hours before: Don't you fear fear?

'But you must go back there, Perseus,' Athena continued. 'Now, while daybreak has hardly arrived, and your victim lies in dreams. Medusa is the mortal one: she sleeps apart from her sisters, and you know why you must kill her. Not to save face at home. But because you have good on your side. Medusa thrives on hate, suspicion, mean spirits. It will be truly terrible, if she rules over the world.'

As Perseus listened, half-doubting, he rested his eyes on Athena's lance. The goddess frowned.

'Yes, Perseus. Of course I could do it myself. My glory was on offer – to you. Still, you can go home. Go on then. Find your little human niche, lead an ordinary life. Look. There are your wings.'

Perseus pulled himself up and shook his head. He drew his knife from its sheath, and flourished the shield. He would, to his peril, take a sideways glance at death. But Athena's shield was suddenly just a minor asset to Perseus. It was Athena's face, her presence, her supreme poise, that charged and galvanized him with the faith: I could die for this.

Within moments he was aloft, noiselessly wafting over the Gorgons' domain. Soon he saw where they made a den. It was a clearing, strewn with bones and debris, where the ashes of a fire still flapped thin curls of smoke. Perseus turned, not for speedy retreat as before, but calmly to make an approach in reverse, relying on his mirror-shield. Propelling himself backwards and closer to the squalid encampment, he could see in the shield's curve two shapes slumped side by side, close to the smoking hearth. Their bodies rose and fell with regular motions. Good: those were the sisters, asleep together as expected. Perseus did not examine them any closer, but quickly angled his shield around until he found another sleeping form. In the grey half-light, clear details were obscure. But nothing had prepared him for the shock of what was lying there. Reflected in silver was the figure of a woman, with her legs spread out beneath the loose folds of a slit skirt. It was a sprawling body, and a powerful one, but in no way misshapen or deformed: rather wondrously symmetrical, even in its relaxed state. As for the head – once, when a small boy, Perseus had come across an animal left dead in the fields, and had seen with morbid amazement how the skull seethed with lice: insofar as he imagined Medusa's face at all, he had thought it might be something deathly alive like that. But set off by a rich cascade of dark hair was a mask of exquisite composure, as if smoothed from cool crystalline marble. The eyelids were closed, and lips set in a tight line, neither grimace nor smile.

Perseus pulled a deep breath, and twisted himself, so that he might approach with his knife poised while still keeping a reflected view of Medusa's flat-out form. He felt nausea beginning to gorge inside him, but this was not the sickness of fright. It was closer to self-loathing. Athena, he wanted to ask, where is the glory here – sneaking towards an unconscious and seemingly harmless woman, and stabbing her pale white throat? But as he hovered into striking distance his resolve was quickly fired. First, he realized that the dark mass of hair was vibrant because it was a headful of black-skinned snakes, each one quivering and alert. Then, perhaps because the snakes were stirring, Medusa opened her eyes. Though it was bounced off by the shield, the look she shot at Perseus was one of such immediate, pitiless hate that impulsively he lunged to save himself. His dagger tugged into the soft ground once, then twice, but he kept his eyes averted. Hands clawed furiously at his wrist, a myriad of angry fangs were spitting about him, and above terrible screams from the Gorgon, Perseus heard the gargled torrent of his own shouting. 'See who dies,' he yelled, and he hit her. 'Damn your eyes!' as he struck again. The knife went through sinews as if through soft cheese. With two blows Medusa's head was lolling askew, the snakes gone flaccid. Perseus dropped the shield, closed his fist round the snakes, and soared up. He knew there was commotion below, as Medusa's sisters howled and hurled curses at him; he knew that his arms were wet not only with the Gorgon's blood but also his own. But he must fly, only fly.

He was still short of breath when the shaggy shoulders of Atlas came into sight. Then he slowed, and allowed himself some triumph. 'Look who I found!' he called out. The Titan peered towards the object Perseus was brandishing. A stricken expression cracked across his face. 'No!' shouted Perseus, wrenching the head in another direction. But it was too late. Atlas gaped, and kept gaping, as strata of granite rippled along his limbs. Perseus could only watch as the weary upholder of the skies became like a lumpy column, which rocked awkwardly – then slid down with a massive crash.

Perseus had been right: when Atlas crumpled and lay as a mountain range, the skies stayed up just as they were. But now Perseus was aghast. No one had warned him that the Gorgon, though dead, would retain the power of her fatal gaze. He shook: he might so easily have taken a glance at her himself. He must descend at once, and parcel up his prize. Then what was he to do with it? The head was pledged to Polydektes. But much as Perseus loathed his future stepfather, he did not wish the absurd little man turned to stone.

Perseus drifted down thoughtfully, holding Medusa's head at a nervous arm's length. He came to a hot land where palm trees sprouted wherever there was water, or cool breezes prevailed. Some weary local farmer, dozing under foliage, reported what could only have been a remarkable religious experience: an angel had dropped from the heavens, and made for his satchel, in which a day's food was stored; had gesticulated wildly, while tipping out the food; had stuffed into the satchel what appeared to be a woman's head; then flown away . . .

Once Medusa's head was safely stowed in the rustic bag, Perseus resumed his homebound course, heading eastwards along the coast. But he had not gone very far before he came across a sight that could not be passed over. Strains of female crying reached him, and looking down he saw that they came from a rocky little island. A naked girl was standing there, raising her arms in despair; her ankles were draped in chains.

Young Perseus had never seen a black person closely before. He had never realized what a warmly graded colour black could be. As he landed on the rock, he was intrigued, and let his eyes hungrily absorb the girl's broad-featured face, the slender stretch of her neck, her proud breasts and hips, her shining thighs.

She tried to cover herself with her hands, and she gave Perseus a look of such reproach and sudden terror that he fell to his knees with shame. The girl understood none of his words, and hers were strange to him. But she pointed across the straits to the shore, as if she meant him to go in that direction, and go quickly. Nothing, he tried to tell her, could be easier. He promised to be back very soon.

There was a settlement on the mainland – a cluster of straw-roofed huts around one large timber hall. Perseus thought it wise to approach the village on foot. Arriving, he was greeted by people evidently of the same tribe as the girl who was chained to the sea-dashed rock. They escorted him to the central hall, festooned with jangling bronzes, where a scribe was found who could understand what Perseus said. An

audience was then arranged with the king: an enormous per-
spiring figure sprawled on a tasselled couch in the company of
six equally plump and languorous women.

Fanned by his concubines, the king munched fruit while
Perseus explained why he had come. The king looked Perseus
over, and shrugged. Perseus then learned that it was the king's
own daughter, Andromeda, who was exposed to the waves;
and that she was put there as a sacrifice, to atone for her
father's boast.

'What was that?' asked Perseus.

The interpreter shuddered. 'His majesty – may he reign forever! – declared that his wives were more numerous and more
beautiful than the maidens of the sea . . . '

'And so?' demanded Perseus, flashing a glance of contempt
at his majesty.

'Ah, and so,' moaned the scribe, 'the lord of the ocean has
vowed to send a monster of the deep, at sundown, to devour
the princess.'

At this point the king emitted a loud belch, and made some
weary remark.

'His majesty – may he reign forever – says that any man
who can save Andromeda shall have her as his bride.'

Perseus drew out his dagger. 'I will do it,' he announced to
the king, ' for her sake, not yours.'

The king peered incredulously at the slender weapon flourished before him; made a remark to his concubines, then sank
back with laughter.

'What's so funny?' demanded Perseus.

'It was an undignified observation which I will not trans-
late. You see', said the interpreter, 'how mighty we are in arms.'

It was true. There were stacks of massive shields and spear-
shafts all around; and great-chested guards standing about
who towered twice the height of the youthful Perseus.

Perseus nodded. He was tempted to twitch his heels and rise up tauntingly. But instead he bowed and left, and did not take flight till he was clear of the timber palace.

The crowds that gathered on the beach as sunset became imminent could barely see the rock where Andromeda was tied. Warriors with their canoes were paddling about in the shallows, but none dared take up the challenge issued by the king: to go forth and confront the beast from the ocean's depths. They had heard tales of its size, its scaly skin, its vast jaws. And sure enough, as the skyline was dipped into purpling pink, so increasingly huge waves began to roll up and slap on the sand. The onlookers shrieked as an enormous horned head appeared out at sea, and was now surging towards Andromeda's rock. Then there was a thrashing, and much spume sent up, as the creature seemed to be distracted by an unidentified flying object circling above its horns, and darting down as if to sting or prick its neck. The monster plunged this way and that, giddying around; then, with a roar that shook the ground under everyone's feet, it sank from view. The waves calmed. Someone who had shinned up a palm tree claimed he could now see two figures on the rock – embracing.

The king himself waddled into the waters and boarded a capacious canoe, and a small flotilla sped across to cut Andromeda free, and bring her back – with the salty but satisfied Perseus. A feast was ordered in the king's hall, and for much of the evening Perseus basked in the glow of tribal celebration. As requested, he had removed his sandals and left his knife at the door. From time to time, however, he noticed some of the king's warriors glowering in his direction, and muttering amongst themselves. The drinking continued, but the atmosphere only grew more tense. Suddenly all the womenfolk, including the sleek-limbed Andromeda, had faded away. The king's scribe, sitting beside Perseus, began to look worried. The king rapped his cup on his plate, and addressed Perseus in slurred but stern tones.

The king was impressed by his valiant spirit (the scribe hastily related) but wished to know how many head of cattle, sacks of flour and ingots of copper his prospective son-in-law had to offer.

Perseus replied candidly. He possessed, he said, no more than what was in the bag he had by his side.

The king's eyes goggled. Then he relaxed into a deep chuckle, and snapped his fingers. Instantly, all the warriors rose to their feet and filed out of the door. The scribe yelped and scurried away. For a few moments Perseus and the king were alone in the torchlit room. The king beamed at Perseus, and passed a chubby forefinger across his throat – the unmistakable signal of . . . You're going to die. Perseus softly reached for his bag. *That's what you think.*

At a signal from the king, the warriors returned with their weapons; they formed a humming, drumming circle around Perseus, the sweat glistening on their knuckles as they came closer and closer, clutching spears. Then Perseus stood up. He displayed what he had in his bag; revolving it to each assailant in turn.

The humming and drumming reduced by degrees – till utter silence ruled. Again, the king and Perseus were the only ones in the hall – the only ones alive. Perseus carefully replaced Medusa's head in the satchel. He poked one of the stone-struck warriors; it wobbled, then thudded to the ground. The king on his couch was speechless, stupefied with disbelief. Perseus, too, said nothing. He collected his sandals, retrieved his precious knife – and soared away by starlight.

The islanders of Seriphos were still in slumber when Perseus returned. All was prepared for the wedding, the next day, of Danae and Polydektes. Polydektes snored with the deep contentment of knowing that numerous guests, distinguished people, had already arrived from all over Greece. Perseus crept into his mother's room, and kissed her cheek; she smiled dreamily. But Perseus was not ready for bed. He went into temple precincts and prayed for Athena to come.

The goddess softly appeared. 'You got it,' she said. 'I knew you would.'

Perseus passed her the bag. 'Please. Take it. Before I freeze or petrify the whole world.'

Athena took it, and peeped inside. 'Don't worry,' she said. 'We can annul Medusa's deadly gaze. I shall find a way of wearing it, though; as a pendant, perhaps. Yes – that might be rather striking. Thank you.'

'I'd better return these, too,' said Perseus, slipping off the winged sandals. 'But I had to drop the shield. Sorry about that.' Perseus lapsed into misery.

'Well, my youngest hero,' Athena went on. 'Are you ready to show us what you're really made of, tomorrow?'

'Haven't I?' said Perseus, hunched in discontent.

'You've just parted with your trophy. Who'll believe your deed? You'll be mocked – and by no one more than Polydektes.'

'I know,' sighed Perseus.

'Then let them,' said Athena. 'The truth will be plain, in due time – and all the more splendid for that. Anyway,' she added, 'the day is your mother's. All she wants is to see you there and smiling. Her father abandoned her. Don't let her son do the same.'

Perseus obeyed the goddess. As Athena predicted, there was much chaffing and amusement at his expense. But he endured it with good humour, simply saying that Medusa no longer existed – so would Polydektes accept a fat ox instead? Danae thought to herself: *My boy has been gone for just a day, but he has come back older by years.*

And certainly Perseus could not be blamed for the one incident that marred a happy day. A festival of games and sports had been organized by Polydektes, to show the visitors from afar what fine physical specimens were nurtured by the island of Seriphos. Polydektes himself took great glee in starting the races, awarding the prizes and so on. He could not resist, however, one further opportunity to humiliate his new – and apparently reformed – stepson. When he announced the list of those taking part in throwing the discus, he added the name of Perseus. The spectators were as surprised as Perseus was himself: the boy cut a very lithe figure next to the muscular hulks who were flexing themselves for the event. But Perseus remembered Athena's words, and accepted the challenge with bemused grace. When it came to his turn, the bronze disc looked so unwieldy in his adolescent hand that the crowd tittered, and pressed forward to witness this hilarious sight. Some stood impudently where the other competitors had already pegged their distances, jeering and nudging each other.

Perseus swung back his arm. He felt strangely at ease: as if he knew his life would turn with this one fluent motion. The disc spun from his fingers; a hiss of admiration went around the field; and moments later, one of the mocking onlookers lay flat in the grass, killed instantly where the weight had come down on his head.

Who was it? Who else but an elderly man who had come to the wedding with not the slightest awareness that he was the father of the bride. Danae had yet to lift her veil. But she, of course, recognized him as the same Akrisios who had cast her away in the wooden chest. So it transpired that Perseus had indeed split the skull of his own grandfather.

Perseus, as everyone agreed, bore no blame. But the rules of the community applied all the same. The guilt of family bloodshed lay with Perseus: he must leave the island.

On Seriphos, to this day, there are many tales of where Perseus went. Some claim he travelled east, and created a clan of people like himself, always itching to move, living only with what they could carry in knapsacks and saddlebags – the ancestors of a great race, the Persians.

Others say he retraced a route to the west, and married a burnished beauty of Ethiopia called Andromeda. She never asked what Perseus brought with him. She knew what he was worth.

# JASON AND THE ARGONAUTS

They told him to go to a land – a land where the sun rises and the rainbow has its end.

These, as he pointed out, were not precise navigational instructions. Did the land have a name?

Colchis.

It meant nothing to him. But then Jason hardly cared where he went – so long as he went with his one true love. She was his only darling. To touch, to trust, to know that in every circumstance – there she was. She wanted nothing more than guidance and caressing. She creaked but never cried. She was his ship, the Argo.

Jason rarely left her helm. The tiller was worn smooth from his palms. As all those who saw the Argo, or served on her, would agree: she was a splendid craft. Her keel cut clean. When all the oars struck well, and her sails were full, she hardly touched the surface. Flying along on board the Argo, then, anyone might believe tall pines grew towards one end – to be cut down and planked, warped and sealed, to go skimming over the deep.

Sometimes Jason simply pressed his nose against the Argo's hull. She had, for him, the resinous scent of home.

It happened like this. There was a king of Thessaly, Pelias, who should not have been king. Pelias had seized the throne from Jason's father, whom he kept behind bars. Jason's mother acted fast: she despatched her baby boy for safety to the deep forested glens of Mount Pelion, where an old centaur, Chiron, agreed to raise the child. Chiron was fierce at first. But he taught Jason many things, breeding him for the hero's part – above all, of course, not to be afraid. A coward, said Chiron, dies many times, a brave soul only once. Coming of age, Jason left the thickets and headed towards home. He intended to avenge the wrong done to his parents. Yet Jason was dressed in forest pelts; he did not cut the figure of a prince. He also lost one sandal on his way. When he came to the court of Pelias, even before he had announced himself, the king took alarm and went into council. Pelias emerged from his consultations beaming. Jason's arrival, he said, had been prophesied. Jason was the one-sandalled hero who was destined to redeem the kingdom from a curse. The curse lay with a miraculous sheepskin. This 'Golden Fleece' was to be found in the far-off, unknown land of Colchis – home of dawn and rainbow's end.

Jason was educated in woodlands, not in the ways of the world. He trusted what Pelias told him. He must return to the mountainside, and lop down timbers for a boat. Then he must assemble shipmates, find this Golden Fleece, and bring it back to Thessaly. So – Pelias affirmed – Jason would restore his family's rights, with immediate effect.

Pelias gave Jason half the truth. He had indeed heard prophecies, the most worrying of which was that the old pretender should one day lose his life to a young man who came with a single bare foot. The story about the curse was his invention; but not the Golden Fleece. It existed, sure enough, in distant Colchis. But it was guarded by forces that defied all mortal assault. If Jason ever found his way to

Colchis, and got close to the Golden Fleece – it was certain death.

Pelias happily sponsored the commission of a fifty-seater vessel, and encouraged Jason to gather the most great-hearted companions for the expedition. Making a list of his own actual or potential enemies, Pelias even suggested names. With any luck, he thought, all fifty of them might disappear on a single voyage . . .

So Jason became proud captain of the sleek, fresh-seasoned galley he named the Argo; and while she was provisioned, he registered his crew.

They came from far and wide. Some knew very well where the journey's purpose lay. Others simply drifted along with nothing better to do. Jason stood at the dockside, logging their names. He was vaguely perturbed about keeping discipline once at sea. Yet each of these would-be 'Argonauts' seemed perfectly sure of a place on board.

Among the first arrivals were two strapping lads. 'We're twins,' they declared, perfectly in unison. 'Castor and Pollux. From Sparta. The Dioskouroi, we are – the double boys. That's us.'

Jason looked from one to another. He could not tell them apart; but both looked like they might be handy in a brawl, not to mention with an oar. He let them embark.

Next came a fine-featured young man who gave his title as Peleus, prince of the Myrmidons.

'Any relation,' queried Jason, 'to Pelias who calls himself King of Thessaly?'

The young man shuddered. 'On the contrary,' he said, very firmly – and proceeded aboard.

Amongst the next batch of volunteers was a stocky, bearded figure who wore what looked like a lion skin draped over his shoulders. He was accompanied by a slight and winsome youth who had dainty curls about an innocent face.

'Now you,' said Jason, '– d'you know, you could almost pass for Herakles, in that outfit?'

'I am Herakles,' said the older man, gravely.

Jason's mouth dropped.

'We were travelling this way, my small friend and I. We thought we might help if we could. This is my squire, Hylas.'

The pair went up the plank.

Later he was confronted by a more unusual couple. One was a beautiful youth, whose face wore an expression of remote doom. The other was a tall, equally striking girl, whose blonde hair was plaited tightly behind her. She wore a long skirt that was slashed up both sides, showing glimpses of firm tanned thighs. The youth stayed sombre, seemingly too downcast to utter anything. It was the girl who addressed Jason, in booming tones.

'Look here,' she said. 'We heard about your call for help to find the Golden Fleece, and we think it's a tremendous jaunt. My name's Atalanta. He's Meleager. Both from Calydon. You might have heard of us. We're first-rate hunters. When do we sail?'

Jason waved her away. 'I'm sorry. It can't be done. The rules are clear. No women among the ranks. Now – who's next?'

Next moment he found himself gripped by the throat and lifted off his heels. Atalanta held him there like a doll as she spoke again. 'Would you mind just repeating that?' she said, coolly. 'We didn't quite hear.'

'I said –' Jason kicked out; and then squealed, as another powerful hand gripped his testicles. Slowly, he was let down.

'I said,' he gasped, '– I said – welcome, Calydonians.'

'Good man,' said Atalanta, breezing ahead.

'You are such a bully,' said the mysteriously sad youth, following her.

Watching this scene with soft brown eyes was another young stranger. He was not swaggeringly handsome, nor packed with muscles and bravado. He carried no weapons: only a tortoise-shell lyre. Jason, still wincing, regarded him nervously.

'And who are you?'

'Orpheus,' said the minstrel. 'Don't worry about them,' he added, with a glance towards Atalanta and her friend. 'There are stories that tell why they are as they are.'

'Is that what you do – tell stories?' demanded Jason.

'Yes.'

'Anything else – apart from smiting the strings?'

Orpheus pondered. 'Not much,' he confessed.

Zeus preserve us, thought Jason. Still: Chiron had taught that nothing matched music for moving the heart. This Orpheus might serve at least to soothe and entertain them all. 'Go on, then,' Jason sighed.

The Argonauts made a motley crew. But almost as soon as the ship left harbour and picked up speed, Jason sensed himself at ease with them all. He sat at the helm, steering their course due east; they were ranged on the benches below, each heartily pulling an oar – except for Orpheus, who took his place at the prow. So long as rowers were needed to cut through the waves, Orpheus kept them in time with his lyre. Everyone sang on the way. At this rate, it seemed, they should be there and back in a week.

Their first port of call was enough to spoil that hope.

The Argo dropped anchor off Lemnos. Unknown to Jason or any of the ship's company, this quiet island was the site of a massacre. For years, the women of Lemnos had endured violence, neglect and betrayal from their husbands. One of the injured, Hypsipyle, had rallied the victims to a drastic response. In one night, all males on the island were murdered. Not even baby boys were left alive. Then the Lemnian women taught themselves whatever tasks their menfolk had assumed – woodcutting, ploughing, infantry drills and more – and soon there was nothing they did not feel empowered to achieve. At first sight of the Argo's sails, a fully armed force was immediately mustered. But Hypsipyle had second thoughts. If her island domain was to flourish, it must be populated. She and her subjects did not desire new husbands, not at all; but they did require a fresh breed of infants. There, on the horizon, was a boatload of potential providers.

So when Jason and a band of companions came ashore in a launch-boat, they were met not with hostility but with an amazingly fragrant welcome. Cool muscat wine was tipped into cups, tables spread with edible delights. Jason and his men could not believe their luck. Girls surrounded them on every side; and not a rival in sight. As twilight dropped, Jason felt the warm weight of Hypsipyle herself settle in his lap. He soon forgot he was the master of a ship at all.

Songbirds were starting when this idyll was disturbed. It was Herakles who had grown impatient and dived off the Argo's side to swim his way ashore. Hearing his far-off shouts, Hypsipyle murmured in Jason's ear.

'There – I hear more of your delicious men. Tell them all to stop with us tonight. We have wine and food – and beds – for everyone.'

Herakles, however, was not in a mood to be seduced. Banging his club on closed doors, he hauled the drowsy sailors out. Herakles had more tact than to upbraid his captain aloud; but as they hurried grimly back to the boat, he muttered his reproach: 'Is this what you call leadership? – not two days on our route, and lost in the arms of a whore?'

Jason was duly ashamed. He made some amends by bringing back with him baskets of fruit and casks of wine offered by Hypsipyle. But he resolved that from then onwards his mission to gain the Golden Fleece would outweigh any personal pleasure of his own. As the sails of the Argo filled with a favouring breeze, he confided as much to Orpheus.

'Are you sure,' Orpheus mused, 'you want the tragic hero's role?'

'Why must that be?' Jason asked.

'Duty over love: what else but tragedy?' replied Orpheus.

'I shan't *be* in love,' said Jason.

'You never know,' said Orpheus, 'when Eros might strike.'

The two men looked down along the Argo's deck. With oars at ease, it was a scene of rest and recreation. Some Argonauts were stripped and sunning themselves; others played at dice, or whittled arrow-shafts. Two sat simply hand in hand: Atalanta and Meleager, the pair from Calydon.

'There,' said Jason, placidly observing them. 'See how Eros gets it right.'

'Does he now?' said Orpheus. Then, softly, the poet told Jason how this love was destined to end.

Returning home from the Argo's voyage, he predicted, Atalanta and Meleager would join a local hunt for a mighty boar, organized by Meleager's uncles – two brothers on his mother's side.

'Firing her bow,' Orpheus went on, 'Atalanta is first to hit the beast. Meleager and his kinsmen close in with their spears; and brave Meleager makes the final kill. He declares his beloved Atalanta as heroine of the chase, and dedicates the boar to her. But this angers the two uncles, who claim the bristling trophy for themselves. There is a quick and violent dispute, as the older men set about Meleager. But Meleager leaves them both dead.'

'As he should,' Jason said, intrigued. 'So what?'

'What you don't know,' said Orpheus, 'is that when Meleager was born, a heaven-sent message came to his mother –
that her boy's life would last only so long as a certain piece of
timber in her fireplace stayed unburned.'

'Really?' said Jason. 'What did she do?'

'As anyone would – leapt to the hearth, pulled out the
smouldering log, doused it in water and hid it away. But –
when she first hears news of her brothers' death – before the
hunt itself returns, before she knows the facts – what do you
think she does?'

Jason shuddered. 'No,' he said. 'She couldn't – what mother
on earth could do that to a son . . .?'

'She does. She will,' said Orpheus, '– retrieve the old brand,
and throw it on the fire. And as it catches light, so Meleager,
far away, stumbles in his tracks; and very soon he is no more.'

Jason got up. 'Right,' he said, purposefully. 'I shall go down
and tell him, immediately, that he must never, never hunt
boar with his uncles –'

Orpheus held him back. 'No. No. You can't.'

'But he could avoid his ghastly death – if only he knew!'

'He can't be made to know,' ruled Orpheus. 'It is what the
future holds. It is what will be.'

'Then what's the use of knowing?' demanded Jason.

'I wonder myself, sometimes,' sighed Orpheus.

Jason gazed away to their starboard side. The Argo was now
gliding quite close to the coast. It was steep-sided here, covered with dense scrub. The rocks and vegetation offered little
invitation to come ashore. Jason noted one or two sandy coves
as they passed, but dismissed any thought of landing there;
tranquil as it seemed, this was perfect terrain for an ambush.

Orpheus seemed to read his mind. 'For example, I have a
strong foreboding about this place. Some time, perhaps hundreds of years from now, men from far away will disembark

here – from ships made of metal – to be cut down like stalks of grass by a scythe. But I can't say when precisely. I don't even know the name of the straits we're sailing now.'

Jason shrugged. 'I can tell you that. For what it's worth. We're in the Dardanelles. There lies a place they call Gallipoli. But Orpheus, really – ships of metal – are you serious? I wouldn't heed your dream. For a start, no commander in his right mind would land an army here.'

To cheer himself up, and to make speed away from this eerily deserted land, Jason organized a rowing competition, in which he took part himself. Other Argonauts joined the challenge of who could row at firm pressure for longest; by the end, though, it was a straight match between Jason and Herakles. Both were pulling hard, the veins standing out on their arms and temples, when there was a loud crack, and Herakles fell back off his seat.

Cursing, the hero examined his fractured oar. 'I could have gone on for hours at that pace,' he growled.

'I believe you,' Jason panted, 'and we can hardly do without you either. Let's anchor here, and make repair. We need water replenishing too.'

The shoreline looked more kindly now, though still there were no signs of habitation. A detachment of Argonauts, including Herakles and his valet Hylas, paddled to land. Herakles went roving for some suitable lumber for his new oar. Finding a good straight conifer, he simply applied a wrestling lock and tugged the tree out by its roots. Then he ensconced himself on the beach, and happily wielded an adze, stripping the bark and planing the wood to the shape of a champion's blade.

By late afternoon his carpentry was done. Others in the party had gone off with their pitchers to find sources of fresh water. Evidently they had scattered in various directions, for they began to come back singly or in pairs. Herakles enquired how it was, further inland. They said it was safe and unpeopled. 'Anyone seen Hylas?' Herakles asked later, as more returned, and the first chills of dusk were descending. Yes, it seemed the boy had been sighted, threading his way towards a tinkling spring. 'I know what'll have happened,' said Herakles, indulgently. 'He'll have filled the jars too full – knowing how thirsty I am. Now he can't manage to carry them home. He's such a good lad. I'll go and find him. We shan't be long.'

Herakles headed off to where Hylas had last been seen. The others waited. They listened to the distant cries of Hylas! Hylas! through the darkening forest glades. Then suddenly the voice of Herakles could be heard no more. For a while they waited, expecting at any moment Herakles and his curly-haired companion to come trudging down to the sand.

'Something's amiss,' said one at last. 'The boy wasn't far away.'

Several of the water-fetchers retraced a route into the woodland. They found Herakles muttering to himself, swiping fistfuls of foliage, at the site of a small, fern-fringed pool. Of the two large earthenware pots that Hylas had borne to the spring, one stood filled to the brim – but the other lay empty on its side.

Herakles was both sweating and ashen-faced. His face was creased with despair; his voice cracked in agony, as he howled up to the heavens.

*'Why? Why must I lose everyone I love?'*

For several hours the search went on. The entire crew of the Argo disembarked, lighting brands and beating tracks through the undergrowth. Eventually, Jason gathered them all back on the beach, under the midnight stars, and declared a halt. He put his arm around the heaving shoulders of Herakles.

'Good Herakles. Don't blame yourself for this. It's a mystery to us all; but, for sure, Hylas is gone from here – and we must move on.'

'You must,' agreed Herakles. '*You* must. Not me.'

With that, Herakles shouldered his club, and turned away. Soon his hunched figure had disappeared inland. The company strained their ears; beyond the thin nocturnal throb of crickets in the dunes, they heard it again – now more a lament than a call:

'*Hylas! Hylas!*'

'I say. That's a shame,' Atalanta said.

Jason nodded. His main regret, though, was losing not Hylas but Herakles. Once he had weighed anchor and resumed the ship's course, he sought counsel from Orpheus.

'Please tell me that mighty Herakles would have been more hindrance than help – in the end.'

Orpheus smiled. 'Indeed he would have been. Because Hera hates him still, and his trials are only halfway through. Havoc, I'm afraid, is habitual to him.'

'I see.' Jason brooded. 'And I don't suppose you understand what happened to that poor little helpmate of his?'

Orpheus bent over his lyre, and caught a chord. 'That,' he said, 'you don't want to know.'

'Yes I do.'

'*The one that rocks us at the knees; lights fires beneath our ribs . . .*' crooned Orpheus, as if to himself. Then, sensing Jason's impatience, he added: 'There are nymphs that live in forests of old. Lovely, long-haired girls. Girls dressed in columbines. Girls who peep from oak leaves. Dryads, naiads – they've all sorts of names and hidden ways. And some flow in the streams and pools.'

Jason was scornful. 'Oh yes? I was brought up in the woods. I never saw such a creature.'

'Bad luck, perhaps, for you. Normally they're mortal-shy. Sometimes, though . . . sometimes they can't resist us. Or we can't resist them – if we so much as catch a glimpse.'

Orpheus lapsed into reverie. 'Hylas was a very lovely boy. I can't count on that. No – with me it will be songs that lure them out.'

Jason gave a derisive snort. 'Enough, enough!' he called as he stamped away.

There, said Orpheus to himself; I knew you wouldn't want to know. Eros –– Eros strikes once more. Beware, my captain, beware.

Orpheus was gifted with insight. But – as he was first to admit – he did not know everything. In some areas he was woefully ignorant. It was Jason, for instance, who opened the poet's mind to the night skies: teaching him how, instead of gawping at the canopy of far-off light-buds, one might seek out single stars, such as Sirius and Arcturus, like old familiar friends; and, rather than feel bewildered by the sparkling assembly of stars, how to plot a position anywhere on sea or land by the astronomic patterns made above – by Orion, the Pleiades, and more.

Geography, too, lay beyond Orpheus. So it was fortunate that the Argonauts, labouring on their easterly course, came to the lands of a king called Phineus, in Thrace. For although Phineus was blind, he knew exactly the route for reaching Colchis, and was happy to speed Jason's mission to retrieve the Golden Fleece. He dictated instructions, which Jason memorized. All were precise and practical, except the last: Heed Aphrodite's laws. This Jason did not understand, and so shut it from his mind.

As Phineus warned, the imminent danger for the Argo's stalwart hull was getting through the Bosphorus – the narrow channel leading to the waters of the Black Sea. It was treacherous to navigate: a jagged avenue made by the Symplegades – 'the Clashing Rocks', as they were known – whose reflex was to close when anything moved between them. Thanks to Phineus, the Argonauts took the precaution of capturing a cormorant before they tried to make passage. The bird was sent skeetering ahead of the ship's prow; the Symplegades clapped shut, nipping its tail feathers, then opened again, and the Argo shot through at full speed, before the rocks could respond. Now they were headed for Colchis, on the far side of the Black Sea – in the land which would become known as Georgia. But what would the heroes accomplish when they arrived?

So long as Colchis was unknown and remote, neither Jason nor his crew had given much thought to what awaited them there. Now, as they approached, their fears began to grow. Colchis was no dreamy outpost at the rainbow's end, but a large and populous kingdom, proudly ruled by one who claimed he was an offspring of Helios – the Sun's own son. Aeetes was his name; and by all reports, Jason could expect no friendly welcome at his court – quite the opposite, if he declared his quest. The Golden Fleece may well have come to Aeetes by illegal means. But since the king possessed it, he used it as a symbol of his solar right to rule.

Before docking at Colchis, the Argonauts conferred. It was Peleus, prince of the Myrmidons, who restored their morale. Yes, he said, Aeetes was formidable indeed, and they could barely hope to match him in force. But no one had ever supposed that the Golden Fleece could be seized by force. Cunning and knowledge were needed here. If Aeetes was as fierce as his reputation claimed, then he must have enemies at home; those among his own people who would be only too glad to see the Argonauts prevail. So Peleus concluded, nodding to Jason. This, then, was the captain's task.

Jason duly presented himself, alone and unarmed, to the court of Aeetes. Aeetes was intimidating enough – scowling and sour, in profile like some great eagle – but Jason spoke courteously and reasonably, pointing out his birthright to the Fleece; but also suggesting ways in which he might recompense the king for its return, and even proposing a temporary loan, if return were not possible.

Aeetes listened in silence. His instinct was to have this smooth-talking Greek buccaneer whipped and thrown into the sea – perhaps with his tongue lopped off for good measure. But then it occurred to him that some sport might be had. To the astonishment of his courtiers, Aeetes told Jason that he conceded the claim. Jason beamed: this ferocious monarch had a heart after all. 'However,' Aeetes went on, 'you will appreciate that ownership of the Golden Fleece is deserved. Such a precious thing cannot be just traded, like some greasy bale of wool – agreed?'

Nervously, Jason agreed.

'So,' said Aeetes, winking at his courtiers, 'let us see you deserve it. A simple agricultural task. One I'd happily do myself. Can you plough? Good. Then take these seeds.' The king reached for a small bag by his throne, and tossed it to Jason.

'There is a field not far away, set aside in honour of Ares – the god who protects this realm. I want you to till its earth and plant what I have given you.'

Jason opened the bag. It was full of teeth – or rather, the yellowed fangs of some large and venomous snake.

'Those came from your part of the world,' Aeetes said. 'Interesting relics. They produce a most curious crop.'

'What would that be, sir?' ventured Jason, half-guessing the answer, and painfully aware that he was now the object of general entertainment.

'Worry about that when the time comes. You may not get so far. You see, a field of Ares can only be tilled by special beasts.' Aeetes paused. 'You'll find them browsing there. Two bulls of bronze – fashioned by Hephaistos. You'll need to put them under the yoke. Take care, Greekling: those bulls breathe fire.'

Aeetes sat back in his throne. The air of amusement suddenly evaporated. 'Now get out of my sight.'

Jason backed away, bowing. He would maintain impeccable deference, though he felt sure he had just been condemned to death.

His dignity under duress, however, did not go unnoticed.

One of those who watched Jason present himself at Colchis was the king's only daughter, Medea. Tall and dark-haired, she had something of her father's superb and commanding presence. But from the very definition of her face, and the way she held herself, anyone could see that Medea was none other than Medea: a determined, independent spirit.

Then Jason arrived.

Was the princess awaiting her chance to make an escape from Colchis? Or was devious Eros simply making an assault on her heart? In any case, no sooner had Jason come into her sight than Medea burned for him, with a snaking, rapid fire. While she listened to Aeetes set the task, Medea knew that it was not for the Golden Fleece. It was the trial to which Jason must submit if he wished to marry her. As she watched how he took the challenge, unprotestingly, she told herself: of course he would; he wanted her.

What did it matter, if they had never met before? They would have years to make amends for that. It was of more pressing importance that the hero prevailed. Dauntless he might be. But he could not overcome this test alone. Medea would help him. Then Jason would see what a true companion he stood to gain.

Jason was back on board the Argo when the messenger

arrived. She was one of Medea's handmaidens, who came breathless and insistent that he step ashore again, by starlight, to meet with one who truly wished him well. Jason followed her.

The sun was fully risen when he returned. He said little to the crew, but they all saw his confidence restored – and the unquenchable delight that brimmed behind his eyes. He sat down by Orpheus; and for some while said nothing at all, simply smiling as he rested his head against the Argo's prow.

'Oh dear,' said Orpheus, after a while. 'So they cut out your tongue, after all.'

'Shut up,' murmured Jason – lost in bliss.

'You only have to confirm. In single syllables if you wish. Was it Medea?'

'Yes.'

'Splendid girl?'

'Yes.'

'Does she want to marry you?'

'Yes.'

'Do you want to marry her?'

'She is splendid. She really is.' Now Jason sat forward, clutching his fists with excitement. 'How can I explain . . . look – you could be lost in the mountains with her, and she'd not give up – d'you understand? She wouldn't mope or moan – she'd find berries and honey, make a fire, gather bedding–'

'You mean,' Orpheus interrupted, 'Medea's not the sort to spend her life at the loom.'

'Right.'

'Well. Good for her.'

'Even better,' said Jason, 'for us.' He rose to his feet, the commander restored. 'She's going to help us get the Golden Fleece.'

Jason was primed for the challenge of yoking the two fire-breath-ing bulls. Before he strode out, Medea secretly anointed him, and all of his armour, with a dilution of aromatic oil. 'I know what you're thinking,' she said, as she knelt down and sprinkled the mixture over his feet: 'How can a mere potion protect me from two flaming and rampaging brutes? My love – trust me. Trust me now, and trust me always. That's all I ask of you.'

Steeped in Medea's charm, Jason strode out to where the field of Ares lay. He had his shield, but no weapons at his side. Upon his shoulders he carried the great oaken yoke to which he must harness the beasts; a deep-slanting ploughshare was trundled along in a cart behind. There was no shortage of spectators for this event. Aeetes was prominent, smirking at the reins of his chariot; all were expecting Jason's swift and violent humiliation – all apart from Medea, who stood at a distance with a small group of royal women.

A massive-timbered paddock contained the brazen bulls. The animals were lying down when Jason approached; but once he had entered their enclosure, they stared angrily at him, and heaved themselves ominously to all fours. Here we go, thought Jason, as each bull began to scrape a hoof on the ground, sending clods of turf flying. First one, then the other lowered its head. Both swayed and breathed hard, issuing explosive sprays of smoke. Then they charged. The gate behind him was shut: Jason had little choice but to hold up his shield against the thundering onrush of hooves and horns.

He expected to be flattened. He braced himself for that end: to be knocked down, trampled, gored and scorched to death in full view of Aeetes and the Colchians. All at once, he steeled his arm, clenched his teeth, and closed his eyes. There was an almighty clang as the bulls impacted on his shield. Jason heard his hair crackle as it was singed by flames, and he felt himself spinning. But when he opened his eyes, he was some-how still upright, while of the two bulls, one was clearly stunned, its forelegs about to buckle at the knees; the other was in an even sorrier state: one horn half-shattered and dangling loose, and a sort of hot black mist steaming from its nostrils. Jason threw aside his barely dented shield and quickly slung ropes around the panting animals. He hauled them together and fastened the yoke. Then he turned, and shouted for Aeetes to bring on the plough.

Spontaneously, there was a burst of applause from the royal retinue – which Aeetes silenced with a roar. The king was astounded, yet furious: Jason's resistance to the fiery stampede defied belief. But the next stage of the contest would finish him off – surely it would.

The bulls were broken, yet strong enough to shamble ahead with the plough. Jason goaded them over the field, sculpting troughs and ridges in the moist dark soil. Finally, he unhitched the beasts, and reached for the little sack of sharp-edged seeds. He walked over the furrows like any farmer would, casting the teeth as he went. Then he picked up his shield, and waited cautiously.

It was someone in the crowd who spotted the first sprout – a shiny crested thing, soon recognizable as a helmet. Similar pointy objects began to proliferate all over the sown field. Then heads appeared – angry, bristling heads, twisting this way and that, as if impatient to begin a fight. Shoulders came next, then the first barbs of spears; and now the heads began to spit and curse. What Jason had raised was nothing less than a brigade of killers, writhing to be free and start some carnage. Aeetes watched in fascinated horror until these seedlings of Ares grew to the waist. Then the king wheeled around his chariot, and galloped away – followed pell-mell by his shrieking subjects.

Jason was stricken with panic. In moments, he seemed to be alone and unarmed in the face of a host that was eager for blood. Already one figure was pulling his feet from the ground, and snarling with long-stored rage. Jason began to back away, wailing for Medea.

Medea was there. As the multitude of fresh-born warriors gained their legs, Jason attempted to run; but Medea laid a hand on his arm. 'Watch this,' she said.

At once she gave a terrible, ear-piercing scream, and pointed to the skies. As if perfectly choreographed, all the advancing figures swivelled to see the cause of alarm. While their attention was turned, Medea deftly stooped for a rock and lobbed it into their midst.

The result was almost comical to watch. The missile struck one soldier in the neck. 'Oi!' he yelled – and swung his fist at the nearest man. As that one sprawled and fell, he knocked over another; who lashed out with his sword, catching yet another with a leap of blood from the throat. Within moments, the entire mob was pitched into close, unremitting combat. Their clashes and death-cries were unbearable to hear. Linking elbows, Medea and Jason walked quickly away. When they looked back, the vultures were already swooping low.

Jason could hardly speak; but Medea had one earnest question to ask. 'I need to know,' she implored. 'Are you a man of your word?'

Jason was offended. Why should she doubt?

'Because my father is not,' Medea went on. 'He lies all the time. He thinks it is a ruler's right to break his word. For instance: he has no intention of letting you take the Golden Fleece, whatever you do to deserve it. And he never even told you that the Fleece is guarded by a monster – did he?'

'A monster?' said Jason, newly alarmed.

'Don't worry. I have a plan.'

Medea halted, and searched Jason's anxious face with her dark eyes. 'My darling,' she said, 'I'll help you – whatever you say. You can leave these shores with your precious Fleece; and think to yourself, years later in Greece, that you once met a girl called Medea – and she loved you with all her heart. Or else . . . you can take me with you. But, please – only if you love me as truly as I love you.'

Jason gripped her strong shoulders. 'I give you my word.'

She pounded his chest with joy; and fell into his arms – where he let her breathe against him.

'Now,' he said gently. 'My amazing, resourceful girl – tell me this plan of yours.'

The monster that guarded the Golden Fleece was a reptile that had survived from deep time. It lay with its body coiled many times in front of a grove, where the glimmering Fleece was suspended from an ancient oak. No mortal had come near the giant snake and survived. Discreetly concealed, Jason watched wide-eyed as Medea walked forward to where the serpent was basking in late-afternoon sun.

Jason strained his ears. Medea was singing as she went – a soothing melody – and moving her head from side to side. The snake shifted and raised its head. A vast mouth opened, and a tongue flickered out. Still Medea approached with her lilting tones. Then Jason saw the trick. As Medea inclined her head this way and that, so the snake began to follow. With one reach of its jaws it might have swallowed her. Instead, it swayed along with Medea's motions. Gradually, as she sang, the monster subsided. Soon it was recumbent. Jason saw Medea holding some herbal sachet by its nostrils, and stroking the beast while she hummed. He sensed a tremor under his feet, and smiled when he realized what it was: a heavy, hypnotized snore. Medea beckoned him out. Jason came across, clambered over the scaly coils, and – reverently, at last – took down from a branch the Golden Fleece.

The Argo was moored at an inlet nearby. Jubilation erupted when Jason came back to the ship with the Fleece draped over his back. Castor and Pollux hoisted him onto their shoulders, to cheers from the exultant crew. Medea watched happily. Though he had hardly done it alone, Jason took all the triumph. She bore no resentment. There, riding high in the eyes of his faithful followers, went Jason – her husband-to-be. That was what mattered to her.

Jason was crowned with a garland of wild celery leaves. Barrels of wine were rolled onto the deck. Orpheus struck up his lyre. The Argonauts settled to prepare for a feast. But the carousing was hardly begun before Medea felt obliged to intervene. She whispered in the captain's ear. Jason, already flushed with wine, scowled and waved her away. Medea was insistent. Jason shrugged, and ordered one of the sailors to climb up the rigging and scan the horizon. The look-out confirmed what Medea had warned. A fleet advancing from Colchis was in sight. With a frenzy of action, the Argonauts abandoned their cups and made ready to leave.

Once anchor was slipped, and the boat picked up speed, Medea joined Jason at the tiller. 'I'm sorry, my love,' she said, '– to spoil your party like that.'

'Thank heavens you did. We would have been trapped in the bay.'

Medea gazed across the waters. Sure enough, there was a flotilla in pursuit.

'What I don't understand,' Jason went on, 'is how you knew. How you know all these things. Putting dragons to sleep – and so on.'

'It's not a secret,' Medea replied. 'I have an aunt called Circe, who lives on an island of her own. I lived with her as a girl. She taught me all I know.' Medea paused, and shook her hair in the salted breeze. 'Some men call her a witch. Those men who don't like any woman knowing more than they do.'

Jason said nothing.

Medea did not notice his silence. 'Now,' she continued, thoughtfully, '– it looks as though we need another plan.'

They did indeed. King Aeetes, determined to stop the theft of the Fleece, had sent his son Apsyrtos to chase the Argo – with instructions also to bring back the princess Medea. Now Apsyrtos was gaining on the Argo fast.

Her ambitious younger brother was not close to Medea. All the same, Jason was taken aback by what she now proposed – which was to lure Apsyrtos to his death. Medea outlined her scheme. A message would be given that Jason was holding Medea hostage, and that he would yield the Fleece, and Medea, plus various other offerings, in return for safe passage home. Apsyrtos must come aboard in person to receive the gifts and make the pledge.

'And then?' asked Jason.

'Use your sword – while I'm talking to him.'

'You'd do that?'

'Yes,' said Medea, 'I would: for you.'

So it happened, by nightfall, out at sea. Apsyrtos, having boarded the Argo in good faith, was about to seize Medea by the wrist when Jason stabbed him from behind. Jason hated the deceit. What he hated even more was how the body was disposed of. Medea wanted her brother cut into pieces, and thrown into the sea as they sailed away to the west. It would delay and frustrate any further chase – for, as she knew, her father would do nothing until he had recovered and buried every part of his precious son and heir.

The Argo pressed on – for Thessaly, and home. On the way, Jason married Medea, promising by all the gods to be faithful unto her. This was a cheerful occasion, spreading light on a troubled and darkening voyage. Even before reaching the land of the old usurper Pelias, they learned that both Jason's mother and father had been murdered since the hero had left to find the Fleece. Jason sank into a deep gloom. Medea acted for him. She stirred an uprising against Pelias from within his own family. In the end it was not Jason who deposed Pelias, but two of the king's own daughters – who had their father killed.

Jason was sickened by it all. He said it was a land of death; he had brought the Fleece to a morgue. He wanted nothing to do with the place.

Medea tried again. She had family ties with the royal house of Corinth; they might find refuge there. So the Argonauts took Jason and Medea onwards to Corinth, where the ship's company was finally dissolved. The Argo rested in dry dock, a sight for tourists to see.

'Could you live here?' Jason asked his wife, as they strolled through Corinth's prosperous port.

Medea squeezed his hand, and said: 'I could live anywhere with you.' And so the couple settled in exile; Jason with no intention ever to return to Thessaly, and Medea content merely to be with him.

It was the poet Orpheus who had said Medea was not the sort of woman to spend her life at the loom. His words were not quite true. Medea could weave as well as anyone. She kept a tidy and pleasant house, soon home to two small sons. It was Jason, not Medea, who possessed the restless nature, and who flouted Aphrodite's laws.

What happened to the couple is painful to relate.

Jason endeared himself to Corinth's elderly king. The king had no sons of his own. One day the king took Jason aside and asked if the hero of the Golden Fleece would care to win a crown. No epic journey required: only that Jason marry into the line of succession.

That was tempting enough. The king's daughter was still in her teens: a pretty, passive, simpering girl, to whom Jason liked to boast of his time at sea – and spin tall tales of how he had fought the ferocious hordes that sprang from Ares' fields, and subdued dragons in their lairs. The girl worshipped him. Jason soon convinced himself to accept the proposal. Medea, he thought, would understand. This was a supreme and irresistible opportunity – his way to power and wealth. Once they were divorced, the royal treasuries of Corinth would be at his command, and he could establish Medea in luxury wherever she might desire. For once, *he* had come up with a plan. He and his former wife would remain friends. Medea would keep the children, and want for nothing throughout the rest of her days.

So Jason reasoned it all. So he told Medea.

First she was speechless. Then she cried: blasted by tears, cowering from a grief that swirled about her like a storm.

She pleaded to him from the wreckage of herself. He failed to pity her. But worse, much worse – he said he did not love her. And, he added – he never had.

Then Medea went very quiet.

He asked if she was seeing sense at last. She said yes – she saw what had to be done. He must be rid of her and the children if he were to become king.

Not 'rid of', he protested. Just – out of the way.

*Out of the way.*

Medea said that she would see what she could do.

He should have known, perhaps. There was no wise Orpheus with him then, to guide the hero in his moves, and teach how passion works. But not even Orpheus might have predicted what Medea's fury would finally demand.

Jason did not find them himself – the little bodies in their beds – limp and cold. They were brought to him by a nurse. He laid them out in daylight, willing them to grow warm again. In his distracted state, he thought he saw a shadow pass across the sun, looked up, and seemed to see Medea there. She was riding a chariot – a chariot pulled by winged gryphons. He cried to her, a cry of eternal hatred. She only flicked the reins, leaving trails of shrill laughter behind.

Jason never became a king – at Corinth or anywhere else. For years he wandered alone in the state of his own desolation. He returned to Corinth to die – hanging himself from the prow of a derelict hulk called the Argo.

Medea, by contrast, became a great queen. She arrived back in Colchis on the day her father died, and was hailed as a saviour sent by Helios himself. Medea made an empire there. She ruled a people known, in her honour, as the Medes.

# III

# WAR ABOUT TROY

# THE JUDGEMENT OF PARIS

All wars have a place of birth. This war was born at a celebration.

It was not a brawl among the guests, or any kind of rumpus like that. The occasion itself was one of solemn joy. The veteran Argonaut Peleus was marking the anniversary of his love for Thetis – the most fetching of sea nymphs that ever sat on a rock and sang as she combed her golden hair. They had been young lovers. Then, while Peleus adventured, Thetis bore him a fine sapling of a son, whom she called Achilles and treasured closely. Returned from all his voyagings, Peleus proposed to confirm Thetis as his wife. He called upon friends far and wide to witness the day. He prayed that the Olympians, too, might bless the festivities. As they did. Poseidon provided a marvellous coach for bride and groom, a carriage built of crested shells and mother-of-pearl. Apollo piped music for a chorus and procession, and the three supreme ladies of heaven – Hera, Athena and Aphrodite – danced along with tambourines. Even toiling Hephaistos left his anvil to take breath and raise a mug of wine to the happy couple.

Only one Olympian onlooker failed to share in the general merriment.

At first Ares watched the proceedings with boredom; then with anger. Joy on earth? Whoever said this was part of the bargain for mortal existence? Happiness was not a right, but a reward. It was time to remind these revellers of that basic law. His fellow deities seemed to have lost their heads. It was left to him, Ares, to reassert divine order in the world.

But, he brooded, he would do so cleverly. Nothing too drastic – just set things in motion; plant the germ of discontent.

He found what he needed in the workshop of Hephaistos. It was an apple made of gold. Ares wondered if he might add it to the celebrations. Hephaistos, banging away, seemed happy enough. So Ares took the apple. But Ares had no intention of making a gift to Peleus and Thetis. Instead, he tied a label to it, and placed the apple prominently on the feasting-table laid out for Hera, Athena and Aphrodite. The mock fruit shone enticingly amid all the edible delicacies there. On the label was simply written: '*FOR THE LOVELIEST ONE OF ALL*'.

Other guests did not notice how the three goddesses all reached for the golden apple at once. It was a discreet quarrel, with seething looks exchanged. But the bickering carried on long after the party had ended. For whom, then, was the gift intended? Eventually Zeus decided that there must be some kind of contest to settle the dispute. He could not possibly judge it himself. An opinion was needed from someone impartial – yet with expertise in assessing the finer points of female pulchritude. Zeus despatched Hermes to find such a suitable authority.

Hermes found Paris.

This Paris was a shepherd. Guarding goats was a somewhat humble occupation for a son of Priam, King of Troy. But – as Paris told himself – the king had fifty children; and only one of them could be reckoned as heir to the Trojan throne. That one, without doubt, was Priam's eldest son, Hector. Clean-jawed, happily married, victorious athlete, gifted rider – and so on: that was Hector. Paris had lost count how far removed he was down the line of royal succession. But Paris did not care. Pastoral life suited him.

Paris could glimpse the walls of Troy – or Ilium, as some called it – through fringes of euphorbia and sinuous asphodels. It was a towering city that occupied a rise in the plains between mountains and sea, at Asia's western edge. But the sight of majestic Troy brought neither pride nor envy to Paris. Invariably he thought to himself: What dross of pomp and busyness behind these walls! While the really important things of life are here in the long sweet grass, warm and ready to hand . . .

And he would squeeze the smooth flanks of whichever girl he had by him at the time.

Paris was – if he put his mind to it – a good shot with a bow and arrow. But he cheerfully admitted to being a thoroughly feckless member of Troy's royal family (and an idle shepherd, come to that). His talent lay in making love. The Trojan hinterland seemed inexhaustibly supplied with nymphs and farmers' daughters – all easily persuaded to spend whole days exploring the dips and contours of their own bodies.

It was in a rare moment without such close company that Hermes invited Paris to act as referee of divine beauty. Even then Paris was relaxed and languorous. 'Can I take off their clothes?' was his first response to the appointment.

'Don't push your luck,' said Hermes sternly. 'Just make a decision, and make it fast.'

So the three goddesses descended to the foothills where Paris lolled, lazily sucking a straw. Each was wearing what she thought to be her most alluring outfit. The idea was that Paris should simply gaze on the trio in turn and deliver his verdict. But none of the contestants could resist tempting him with a bribe. Hera came first, her generous cleavage well displayed in a low-cut gown of deep-green silk. 'Choose me,' she murmured, 'and you, young man, will find yourself to be the richest man in all Asia – and ruler of cities that will make old Troy look like a shanty town.'

Paris nodded respectfully. But to hear what Hera promised did not have him tingling with greed. Big cities? All those meetings, councils, committees, taxes to collect? Hera's breasts were a marvel that he longed to test with his touch. But her prize? Sheer punishment.

Athena came next, and Paris nearly fainted in delight. The goddess strode towards him in a pair of sleek, high-heeled hunting boots, close-fitting up to her thighs; and little else except for a military-style corselet, laced at the back, a proud plumed helmet, and – reduced to the size of an amulet, but unmistakable all the same – the glaring, frenzied head of the gorgon Medusa.

Athena carried a riding crop which she tapped against her shiny boots. 'Why so amazed?' the goddess smiled. 'I exist to be adored. I know you won't fail me. But there is a reward for being a good boy.'

Paris gulped. 'Yes?' he said, eagerly.

'Oh yes,' said Athena, jutting before him. 'I will grant you the powers for glorious victory in every battle you enter. Hector will seem like a limp-wristed coward next to you. Now how would you like that?'

Athena was a magnificent sight. But again Paris felt his heart sink. He had never understood why most men felt obliged to fight in order to prove their virility. Blood, dirt, wounds – nasty. His field of campaign lay in the long grass. The only scars he bore were the bites and scratches of female ecstasy. All the same – as Athena turned and strode off confidently, he yearned to belong to her.

Then it was Aphrodite's turn.

Aphrodite wore a shimmering but simple dress of some

light material. Although it seemed the sort of modest gown a priestess might wear, it both clung to and revealed her swaying shape. Her hair fell loose, also in the spirit of wild innocence. She floated by Paris, brushing him with her skirts; and whispered softly as she came close: *'This is how she is, Paris – Helen, the most exquisite girl in all the world. Pick me, and – she's all yours . . .'*

Aphrodite let the tip of her tongue flicker over his earlobe. Paris shuddered. He knew what desire was. He had desired many women; he desired Hera and Athena. But he had never felt such a seizure as this: as if a hundred hot hard hammers were hitting at his heart, and every innard of his body was leaping for release. There was no time to deliberate. He knew he must have what Aphrodite offered him. He must have it as soon as he could, now, and forever – whatever it took.

Paris could scarcely pronounce his judgement, he was so hungry for its reward. And Aphrodite, enraptured by the victory, was quick to keep her word. She arranged for Paris and Helen to meet, alone. She ensured that they fiercely believed they could not survive a minute if their lives were not shared. So Paris brought Helen to Troy, in the bliss of possessing all he would ever want; and Helen came to Troy, because she would have settled anywhere – so long as Paris was there. She had been admired by men all her days, she had been esteemed, even pampered; but no one had loved her as Paris did, with such tenderness and wonderment.

There was indeed a divine aspect to Helen. She was a daughter of Zeus by Leda, a princess of the city of Sparta. There was no courtship: Zeus came down in the form of an urgent swan, with a flurry of hissing and wings that left Leda breathless but inspired. But Helen knew none of that. She had been raised as an enigmatic Spartan beauty; and in due time, she achieved royal status. For she was chosen as the wife of Menelaus – Sparta's warrior-king.

So Paris had found his perfect match in Helen; but Helen already belonged to another man. And from his vantage point above all this, the god Ares was banging his fists with glee. This could not have been better. Menelaus had the sort of belligerent spirit that Ares approved. He could be counted on for a fierce reaction.

To Menelaus, Helen was more than just a symbol of his own virility. She was a trapping of kingship, a widely envied prize of Spartan power. Everywhere he went, Menelaus heard people telling him that Helen's beauty was all-surpassing. When he hit her (as he did), Menelaus had to restrain himself from leaving bruises on her face: for Helen's face was a marvel that other warlords travelled far to see. Now he was insulted by this squalid act of theft. The challenge to his manhood he might settle alone with the impudent Paris. But this was surely a calculated taunt from an upstart foreign state. Greek honour at large was mocked.

King Menelaus set about rallying his friends to the cause. They were not only to reclaim Helen: all Troy and the Trojans must be punished. The Greeks must assemble a mighty armada of a thousand ships to sail across the Aegean Sea. They should pitch their boats on the beach and ransack the citadel. It would be a lightning strike, except that the Trojans would be left quite clear as to what had struck them: the broad-shouldered vanguard of Greece – heroes from the western world.

The alliance gathered strength. Once Menelaus had persuaded his brother Agamemnon, King of Mycenae, to join the expedition, mustering further support was easy. Menelaus might have a score to settle, but Agamemnon was rich and wise. If Agamemnon deemed Troy a threat to their families and livelihoods, many other Greek chieftains were ready to follow him. A very senior campaigner, Nestor of Pylos, immediately pledged his strategic wisdom to the cause, though he was well past his seventieth year. Young Diomedes, captain of men from the heartlands around Argos and Tiryns, gave eighty ships to the fleet. Another great boon came in the towering form of Ajax, offspring of Telamon – a man who by his very physique suggested a massive joist or pillar, and whose scorn of injury had been proven on the battlefield over and again. And if a killing machine were called for, there it was in the lean young shape of Achilles, the son of Peleus and Thetis. Achilles had spent much of his youth living almost wild among the beechwoods of Mount Pelion, raised on a diet of bone marrow siphoned from lions and deer. He was superbly strong and fast; such education as he had been given came from the same wise old centaur who had tutored Jason – Chiron, who encouraged the boy to think of himself as peerless and extravagant in all that he did. So Achilles was haughty and wilful; but a talisman to those who loved him, and a terror to his enemies. He brought with him a battalion of wiry darting followers, the Myrmidons, who were sworn to obey him and him alone; also his soulmate and cherished friend, the handsome Patroklos.

Not quite every hero in the land, however, was eager to be conscribed. Menelaus wanted to summon the services of one called Odysseus, famous for those touches of stealth and cleverness worth any amount of muscle on the battlefield. But Odysseus had settled down to rule his palace on the island of Ithaca, a small but prosperous domain in the north-west reaches of Greece. He had a newly wed wife, Penelope, and by her, an infant son called Telemachus. Odysseus had heard about the abduction of Helen, and thought it a case of good riddance. Being warned of the imminent arrival of recruiting officers from Sparta, Odysseus exchanged his crown for a battered rustic cap and went out onto his estate, pretending to be a half-witted ploughman – stumbling over the clods, shaking his head and gabbling to himself. But the runners sent by Menelaus saw through the ruse. They grabbed little Telemachus and carried him out to the fields, where they placed his cradle in a furrow right in the course of this senile yokel and his team of oxen. Of course Odysseus dropped the reins and saved his son from being trampled by the beasts. He listened sceptically to the entreaties upon him to sail against Troy. 'Come along,' they urged. 'The crops will grow without you . . . and anyway – we shall all be back for harvest-time!'

Odysseus shrugged. His forebodings told him otherwise. His armour was rusting on hooks in an outhouse. Yet he went to fetch it.

# THE WRATH OF ACHILLES

From the outset, the fears of Odysseus were justified. The Greek fleet assembled on the coast to the north of Athens, at a place called Aulis. The ships came from all over. They looked splendid, thoroughly invincible. But they could go nowhere while their sails hung limp in a breezeless air. Days went by. Not a nudge of wind occurred. The commanders were nonplussed. This was not natural. Some deity was displeased.

As it happened, the Olympians had already taken sides. Supporting the Greeks were Hera and Athena, united by their rankling anger at being spurned by Paris. Hermes and Poseidon also nursed sundry old grudges against Priam and his people. In favour of the Trojans, however, was Aphrodite. She persuaded Apollo and his sister Artemis to join the cause. Artemis, huntress and mistress of animals, remembered that Agamemnon had recently offended her by boasting of his prowess in shooting a stag. It was Artemis who arrested the winds from Aulis.

The expedition's prophet and chaplain, Calchas, divined as much. He told Agamemnon that there was only one way to make the goddess relent. The cost was heavy: nothing less than the sacrifice of his own daughter, Iphigeneia, who had come to Aulis dutifully to wave her father farewell. The other commanders looked on amazed as Agamemnon prepared to do as he was asked. An altar was raised, and Iphigeneia fastened to it. Agamemnon, his face a mask of doubt and grief, poised a dagger over the girl's throat. Only the quick-witted Odysseus saved her. He sprang forward and blocked Agamemnon's arm. 'Hold it, you fool,' he shouted, '– just listen!'

Those gathered by the altar strained their ears. What on earth was there to hear – save some wheezing of leaves in the nearby trees?

'Gods alive,' said Odysseus, shaking his head, 'do I have to spell it out?'

As Odysseus set about cutting Iphigeneia loose, a young deer trotted into the clearing, and nuzzled up to him. 'Ah,' nodded old Calchas. 'Here is what the goddess wants.'

'Now you tell us,' muttered Odysseus. To Agamemnon he said: 'We get the message. This royal muster of force matters more to you than your family. Heaven help *you* when – *if* – we ever get home. Now look – it's blowing eastwards. Let's go.'

So at last the ships slid away from Aulis. But those days of calm had given the Trojans a precious period of readiness to prepare their city for a long siege. Priam had ordered in stocks of grain, and ordered out many of the women and children. The men dug deep cisterns to collect water, and devised tunnels under Troy's giant bastions and walls. Other settlements along the coast were fortified. Priam's son Hector was put in command of resistance to the Greeks. Hector heard that an enormous force of invaders was on its way. He had no intention of giving them the satisfaction of immediate pitched battle. Let them shake their spears at blank masonry till they tired and felt hunger. Then what would they do? The countryside was emptied, crops cleared, barns burnt down. Hector did not much care if this haughty creature Helen stayed at Troy or not. But surrender was not any part of his nature.

From a vantage point on a peak of the isle of Samothrace, Ares watched the Greek fleet cutting across towards Troy. Let either side prevail: so long as there was spillage of blood and wrecking of lives – the more the better, purging the world of its settled habits. Zeus came across his prickly son, now peering across to the Trojan plain where hostilities were due to begin. 'You're looking uncommonly pleased with yourself,' said Zeus. 'Could this be your doing?'

'Me?' protested Ares. 'Not a bit. Just looking at these laughable mortals. We've got to let them have it out, haven't we? How else, Father, will they learn to keep up their respect for you?'

'By knocking out each others' brains?' Zeus wondered. 'Can they not think of gentler ways?'

When the Greeks arrived, however, there was little immediate spectacle for Ares. Agamemnon and Menelaus led an advance party to plan the assault on Troy – and came back to announce that this was going to be a much more formidable operation than any of them, even Nestor with all his experience, had envisaged. A camp was established, and scouting missions sent out. Some skirmishes occurred. But the Trojans stayed safe behind their walls, with supply lines intact: wealthy Priam had seen to that.

Days lengthened, and passed slowly. Discipline among the Greeks, fragile from the outset, began to come apart. Achilles was first to lose patience with the delay of full-tilt action at Troy. He and his battalion of Myrmidons went raiding further along the coast, disappearing for weeks on end. Other commanders, just to keep up morale, took their men inland, seeking villages to plunder. All Greek womenfolk had been left behind, so lonesome men were in search of concubines. In the course of his raids, Agamemnon had secured for himself a slant-eyed beauty named Chryseis, or 'Cressida' to the

Greeks. Then Apollo spread dysentery among the Greek ranks, and the prophet Calchas again called upon Agamemnon to pay the price of leadership: this time, by returning Chryseis to her people. Agamemnon agreed to do so – but only on the condition that he could then take the girl who had been assigned to Achilles. Her name was Briseis: she had bright cheeks, and could sing. It was for her voice – and nothing but her voice, as the troops joked – that Achilles kept Briseis. Agamemnon insisted: as chief-in-command, he was entitled to first choice of captive women. There was a shouting match between the two men; it ended with Achilles angrily thrusting Briseis to the ground in front of Agamemnon, and turning on his heel. Let the chief give orders to a girl, Achilles said: one man was now beyond his authority. With that, Achilles disappeared into his own quarters.

Among those observing this quarrel was Thersites, a menial soldier among the auxiliaries. Thersites was reckoned the ugliest man on the Greek expedition: slack-bellied, with lardy arms, sulky pouches round his jowls, suspicious piggy eyes, and a slick of greasy hair drawn across the balding dome of his head. Still, his voice carried well, and his truculent outbursts often won him an audience with those manning the base camp. After a typical tirade, delivered to a detachment of men set chopping leeks and boiling lentils for yet another meal of vegetable soup, Thersites was emboldened to take his complaints to a higher level. Carrying a bowl of the thick brown mush in his stubby hands, Thersites barracked Agamemnon, Menelaus and the others as they ambled to their regular evening meal of roast meat.

'*Oi!*' he called. 'Oi, you – big cheeses! Why not try something new for supper? I've got a nice thick pot of it right here. Go on, try it – makes you fart like an ox. We should know – it's what we've been living on ever since we got here. But would one of you gentlemen care to tell us what it's all been in aid of? Eh? Call me stupid, but I've never been sure why we ever beached up at this godawful place. Seasons come and go – and it doesn't get more obvious, does it? So what's it all about? Cressida, Bressida – d'you know we don't give a toss which one of you she keeps warm at night? Why not admit it – it's time to go home?'

Thersites got no further. It was Odysseus who raised his stick and cut Thersites short with a flurry of blows about his sloping shoulders.

'Shut up!' shouted Odysseus, between thwacks, '– you useless brute – we all know where you'll be when it does come to action – squirming back in the kitchens, snout in the trough! This,' he cried, snatching up the bowl of soup that Thersites had brought, and tipping it over his frizzy head, '– is all you deserve!'

Squealing Thersites scurried away. But later, as the commanders sat around in their dining tent, over draughts of wine, Odysseus gazed gloomily into his cup, and muttered: *'That odious hog, Thersites – he was right.'* Odysseus was thinking of his only son, Telemachus; and how, with every month and season that passed at Troy, he was squandering a father's time. Since he came, Odysseus had whiled away many evenings by making toys – little wooden horses with neat disc wheels, chin-up warriors brandishing their spears. Now, overcome by nostalgia and remorse, he quitted the company, stamped back to his quarters, and swept those toys away. What were they but – gewgaws that the boy must surely have outgrown?

Inside Troy, that same evening, Hector was deep in conversation with his father Priam. Hector's mother, Hecuba, sat close by – at once pained and proud to see how the siege of their city had silvered Hector's hair. No man could have marshalled a city's defences more tirelessly, assuming every inhabitant to be as precious as his own family. Tonight, however, Hector was sounding belligerent. He had got news of the rifts in the Greek camp. Achilles, they said, was ready to leave; some also reported imminent mutiny among the lower ranks. So far, Hector had kept to his patient strategy of frustrating and teasing the enemy. But at last it seemed to him that the Trojans, though outnumbered, were well placed to launch an offensive and drive their oppressors away. Or better still: to destroy them, on the very strip of land that lay between Troy and the sea.

Priam nodded and gave his blessing. The king did not think to end his days with a view of Greek tents on the plain. Queen Hecuba was more fretful. Of all her many children, none shared Hector's unshakable nobility. She knew that if Hector had calculated he could save Troy by his own death, he would not hesitate to make the sacrifice. Was this what he intended – that his own parents should bury him?

It was not long before Hector pounced on the Greeks. He selected a squad of his most reliable and versatile fighting men – Aeneas and Sarpedon were foremost – and led them out of the citadel under cover of darkness. With faces blackened, the Trojan raiding party crept around the edge of the Greek camp unnoticed. The camp was not their target. Hector wanted to plant panic among those laying siege; he wanted the Greeks to feel they had not trapped Troy but rather were trapped themselves. So let damage commence with their means of escape.

There was a line of defence around the thousand-strong fleet of ships – some hauled onto the beach, others anchored closely offshore – but its sentries had become slack and dozy. The guards hardly had time to yell the alarm before Trojan lances punctured their ribs. Hector himself was first to reach the Greek ships, and he passed swiftly along the upturned keels, daubing each one with a sticky dark mixture he had carried in a barrel on his back. Close behind him came an expert with tinder and flints. A torch was lit. Within minutes, the night sky was opened by flames, and the air made close with smoke – and the muffled, almost bemused grunts of men who died whilst still deep in their dreams. The Trojans moved as a pack. Hector alone left more than twenty men retching in the mists of death. Yet he could not risk being cut off from Troy, and made a retreat before dawn.

Daylight stole on a sorry sight: stark charred timbers, smouldering spars; surf running red on the sand.

Shaking his head as he paced along the shore, Agamemnon barked orders. Overnight he had gone from being lord over an army of complacent occupation to a general harried by the prospect of disaster. He chose a team of officers, headed by Nestor, to seek out Achilles. 'Tell him to grow up – no, correction: to *arm up*, to mobilize. It's no time for selfish games.' The delegation hastened across to the little empire that Achilles had created for himself, his beloved Patroklos, and the Myrmidons. They found Achilles lying on a couch, with his eyes closed, humming as Patroklos bent over a tortoise-shell lyre, plucking old melodies of their Thessalian homeland. With no stinting on detail, Nestor related what had happened: in short, half the ships were left beyond repair.

Achilles lazily opened his eyes, and raised himself onto one elbow. 'You're talking about the ships on the beach, I take it?'

'Indeed.'

'That's all right then,' drawled Achilles, slumping back with a sigh. 'Mine are at anchor offshore, ready to go. We'll be setting sail with the next good breeze.'

Nestor was, for once, almost speechless with indignation.

'What! You'd leave your fellow countrymen to perish here?' he blustered.

'Oh,' said Achilles, 'they're all big boys. They can look after themselves.' He turned to Patroklos. 'Now play on, dear heart.'

Among the ambassadors to Achilles was Odysseus. Up to this point he had said nothing – a silence that was ominous to anyone who knew Odysseus well. He stepped forward.

'Nestor – enough. I know what this is really about. Let Achilles be. He's young. Why should he want to die – die for the sake of another man's wife?'

Achilles sat up sharp; but Odysseus bade him to be easy.

'No, Achilles – there's nothing to say. I'm not accusing you of avoiding combat – though I can't say that meeting Hector face to face fits my idea of a good time. You do as you please. Just know – *that I know.*'

There was a pause. Achilles looked away.

'How about our strumming friend?' said Nestor, nodding at Patroklos. 'Or have his fingers got too delicate to use a spear?'

'Watch your lip, old man –' said Patroklos, rising angrily. But Achilles laid a fond restraining hand on him, and motioned the visitors away. Once they were gone, Patroklos asked Achilles: 'What was that about?'

'Nothing,' said Achilles. 'Just sing to me.'

Outside, Nestor put the same question to Odysseus.

'Ah,' said Odysseus. 'There was a message from the oracle for Achilles. I got wind of it, as you do.'

'As *you* do,' observed Nestor testily.

'Anyway. The prediction was that if Achilles were ever to kill Hector, then his own fate is to die soon after.'

'Bah!' said Nestor. 'I don't believe it. Why – once Hector's dead, there'll be no one left to match Achilles.'

'Who knows?' mused Odysseus.

Back in the tent, Achilles was once more supine on his bed. But Patroklos had put aside his lyre. A horn had sounded around the Greek camp – the signal to muster for action. Patroklos was buckling up. Within a day or two, probably, he and Achilles and the Myrmidon entourage would be gone from this place. Patroklos was happy enough to leave. But first he intended to give just one display of what would be lost to the Greeks when he and Achilles departed.

He gazed at his languid comrade. 'I've taken your armour. I don't know why. I just felt like it. It smells right.'

'Go on,' purred Achilles. 'Just be sure to paint it with anyone's blood but your own.'

The horn had been blown because at last the great bronze doors of Troy were thrown open. With the Greek commanders still at odds, and their forces still shocked by what had happened to the ships, files of Trojan troops were now marching out of the city. They were marshalled by Hector, thundering about in a brassy chariot. To the onlooking Greeks, this was a show of strength they had not expected at all. Where were the ragged, hunger-torn victims of a prolonged siege? How could one beleaguered city hold so many trim ranks of freshly stepping warriors?

The appearance of Patroklos helped to hearten them. He was not Achilles; but just by the way he strode to take a place in the front line, it was clear he intended to deal some damage in this encounter. Cheering, clapping, the Greeks stood aside as he pushed his way through to join the invariable stalwart of every advance, Ajax. Ajax was there with his seven-layered shield, a broadside that most other men could scarcely lift. At the sight of Patroklos, happiness creased across his stubble-dark features. It was a strangely amiable face that Ajax showed to the world, for all that it was ridged by scars. He held out his huge ham of a hand to Patroklos. 'Good man,' he said. Ajax was not effusive with words, and what words he uttered were always short. But he never left anyone in doubt where he stood: foursquare and steady.

Together Ajax and Patroklos took the battle to the Trojans. By the customary rules of engagement, the opposing sides were stationed apart, exchanging taunts and boasts, each waiting for the other to make the first move. Even then, the main body of soldiers would hold back while chosen champions from their lines came forward and did combat one-on-one, to shouts and the clattering of spears on shields. A piper-boy puffed his shrill reeds as Ajax and Patroklos clanked steadily forward, apparently regardless of what stood between them and the gates of Troy. At their approach, Hector wheeled around in his chariot, ordering his men to stand firm. Then he dismounted, and called out to them all.

'Ajax is mine – who'll take the pretty one?'

Several Trojans raised their weapons to volunteer. But Hector's choice was one of his allies from along the coast – the young Lycian prince Sarpedon. Sarpedon joined Hector, and they too advanced across the plain.

Hector's eyes were fixed before him. 'Fight well, friend,' he said. 'As I know you can. No turning away. No freezing of the knees.'

Sarpedon, also looking straight ahead, replied in grim staccato: 'To fight good is good. If Sarpedon fight good and win, at home welcomed as hero. Best place at every feast, cup full of mellow wine. If fight good and die, then Sarpedon family raise mound of earth and bury Sarpedon good, very good – so no one forgets name of Sarpedon.'

Hector nodded. Licking the palm of his right hand, he gripped the shaft of his spear – and with a great cry loosed the weapon. It spun as it went, and ripped into the layers of bronze and bulls' hide that Ajax carried as his shield. Ajax was knocked backwards by the force. Hector gave another vast yell and broke into a run. Then Sarpedon launched his spear at Patroklos. It whistled fast, but Patroklos ducked its path; travelling on, the lance went clean through the throat of a man standing cautiously far behind. Ajax was rolling on the ground, tugging at the spear lodged in his shield, as Hector fell upon him, followed by a mob of Trojans all eager to close in once the big man was down. Yet somehow Ajax rose to his feet. Surrounded, unbudging, with blows coming down on him from every direction, he was like a thick-skinned donkey that has strayed into a field of wheat, still munching at sweet ears of grain while belaboured by boys with sticks. So Ajax stuck his ground till help arrived.

Meanwhile Sarpedon and Patroklos were trading thrusts and cuts. Patroklos kept up a patter of mocking asides.

'What are you doing here, so far from home? Hector got no one else to call up?' he sneered, as Sarpedon grunted and lunged. 'Missed again!' he laughed; and as he danced about, Patroklos flicked his sword at those parts of Sarpedon unguarded by bronze. Soon blood spouted from a wrist; then with a double slice Patroklos neatly caught the tendons behind one and then another knee. Brave Sarpedon tried to stand. He staggered – his face a mask of disbelief – and crumpled to the ground. 'Alas, peasant – not worth the journey,' said Patroklos, flashing a slim gilded dagger before Sarpedon's eyes – and finding a home for it deep in his chest.

Hector, deep in the fray that still clung to craggy Ajax, did not see Sarpedon go down. By the time word reached the Trojan leader, Patroklos had conducted his dance of death around several other unfortunate Trojans. Lost in the ecstasy of his own skilled and whirling swordsmanship, Patroklos noticed too late that Hector was gaining on him. He had just pitched a Trojan from a chariot, and stood back to admire the victim's fall ('*Nice* dive! What style!'), when he felt some intrusion between his shoulder blades. He winced. It was time to retire. But his exit was solidly blocked.

'An elegant farewell,' muttered Hector, 'but farewell all the same –' planting his spear in that part of Patroklos he intended to spoil: the groin. Even as Patroklos collapsed, Hector was already pulling at his plumed casque and smart corselet. 'The armour's nice –' said Hector angrily – 'but where was your boyfriend when you needed him?'

Patroklos resorted to a final smile. 'Oh,' he gasped. '*He'll have you for this.*'

Battle was abroad when the howl was heard – the howl from Achilles when tidings were brought to his tent. It was a tremendous noise. It resounded even on the ocean floor, where the hero's mother knew it at once. Thetis took to her silvery feet; and was there in an instant, to see Achilles rolling amid tears and dust, slapping his head till it oozed with blood. She knelt, a cradle to his curled-up grief. In her lap he subsided. But only to vows of revenge.

'My darling,' she soothed. 'You know what comes next – if you do what you say . . .'

'I want it to come.'

'No, no, don't say that –'

Thetis stroked her son's powerful neck. Even when he was new-born, she had suffered premonitions of his death. She wanted him to be immortal – so desperately that she had taken her baby down to the Underworld, and dipped him in the River Styx, believing it would bring immunity from death. And yet the oracle had made it clear: that if Achilles killed Hector, his own death must follow.

He still seemed such a youth to her; she cried with him, and for him.

Eventually she said: 'Wait till dawn. Even you, Achilles,

cannot kill Hector unarmed. I will be back.'

She knew where to go and swiftly she went. On Mount Olympus; a dark recess, but glowing, noisy and hot. The smell of the place was strong, too, but not unpleasant – reeking of woodsmoke, mastic, fused metal and toil. She paused by its threshold. In the centre of the cave stood a glittering trolley of gold, fixed upon wheels. Dainty and polished, it seemed like a reprimand to all the surrounding clutter and grime. 'Watch this,' coughed the voice of Hephaistos. He bent over the contraption and released a spring. There was a whirring response; then the little cart trundled off across the floor, thoughtfully slowing as it reached the point where Thetis had arrived. She gave an involuntary shriek of delight.

'Moves better than its maker,' Hephaistos growled. He limped over. Then his glare softened. He had not seen Thetis since her marriage.

'How d'you like that little toy? It'll ferry things around – maybe amuse Father Zeus. If those mortals below could contrive such things, how happy their poor mules would be, eh? Wait – now – what's wrong with you?'

Thetis was sobbing. She tried to explain. Achilles would fight. If he lost he would die, if he won he would die. What, then, was a mother to do? She thought there was just one chance. If the armour that covered him were specially made – divinely made – perhaps, then, he might escape his fate . . .

'*Perhaps*,' Hephaistos frowned. His arms were folded sternly: but it was not often that a pretty woman came imploring to his unlovely den. 'When did you say you needed it? You'll be lucky,' he continued, rolling up his sleeves, and fetching a pair of bellows. 'Can't be done, can't be done,' he grumbled, huffing the fire beneath his crucible.

Thetis thought it wise to take a stool in the shadows, and quietly spectate.

It could be done – though only by Hephaistos. Blinking at
the clangs he made, shading her cheeks from the furious
blasts of heat that reached her, Thetis marvelled at the trans-
formations: how lumps of ore were boiled into soup and
ladled into moulds; how other pieces were baked white, then
plied over an anvil with hammer and tongs. Hephaistos
ignored her. He was absorbed in his task, cursing any spillage
or mishap, crooning when all happened as it should. The veins
on his forearms purpled and bulged, sweat ran in channels
down his sooty face. The commission was to produce helmet,
greaves, corselet and shield for Achilles. Each should be splendid, but none more splendid than the shield. This was to shine
like the hero's own huge magnificent medallion: emblazoned
so richly that an enemy might be mesmerized merely by the
sight of it.

Pattering over the roundel with mallet and point, Hephaistos embossed ring after ring of bright relief that stood out
proud and caught the eye. Nothing lay beyond his art. The
heavens were there, with all their constellations; the sun, the
moon, and whatever might happen below – the worst and best
of it. So Hephaistos etched a city of mortals that was a city
under duress: warriors laying siege, armies confronted, bodies
melding into mud and dust. Well-built towers were collapsing
into sighs of smoke; mothers screaming for infants lost; and
long lines of homeless folk dragging themselves to somewhere else unknown. As this misery took shape on the surface of the shield, Thetis clutched herself and wept. The
shield, after all, was an instrument of strife. Her son was not
the sort to keep it hanging spotless on a wall.

But, on the same shield, Hephaistos showed somewhere
else. This was a city that was governed well. Thetis saw meetings and deliberations. There were elders heeding the new
energy of youth, and young people respecting experience.

Traders were supplying what the citizens required, with goods exchanged for what they were worth. Harmony held rule. In the hinterland of this contented place, there was ploughing under way, the dark tilth so moist and keenly carved it seemed to scent the air. Further along came harvest-time, and vintage: reapers stooping to cut, dogs chasing rabbits flushed from the field; binders making stacks, and barleycorn thrown around a threshing floor. There were great wicker baskets heaped with grapes; big-eyed cattle browsing by a river's edge; and tables spread with plenteous food. And then there was the dancing. Women and girls, men and boys, all took their turn as rhythms called. They linked arms, stepping in time, chanting together the tunes that they knew. Thetis found herself swaying along, beating her feet – then blushed when she saw that Hephaistos had now laid down his tools, and was watching her, with the suggestion of a smile written below his crinkled brow.

She glanced beyond: the stars were pale. 'I must go.'

Hephaistos handed her what he had made: using the shield as a bowl.

'I forgot where I was –' she started to say.

Hephaistos shrugged.

'It's my music,' he said, softly. 'Songs – on bronze.'

The armour was delivered before sunrise. Achilles had not slept: he was chafing in his tent. A band of his faithful Myrmidons, all lean and agitated, formed guard around the outstretched body of Patroklos nearby. Thetis was brisk with her son.

'Now do what you must,' she said. 'Leave the dead one to my tending. Go; and come back.'

Achilles needed no bidding. Even as he donned his new accoutrements – still warm from the forge of Hephaistos – he was rousing his fellow Greeks to battle. Ajax, caught champing over an enormous platter of oatmeal, rose to his feet with a groan.

'Sit down, Ajax,' came the measured tones of Odysseus. 'It's too early to fight. Finish your breakfast. Achilles – what will you have?'

'Not hungry,' snapped Achilles. 'Not for food.'

Odysseus coldly stared at him. 'Excuse us for saying it,' he said, '– but Patroklos was not the first to die out here. Give us a break, man. Only fools fight on an empty stomach.'

'I'm feeling foolish,' said Achilles. 'I'm feeling very foolish indeed.' He suddenly shouted, his voice now ringing throughout the camp and beyond. 'HECTOR IS DEAD. DID EVERYBODY HEAR THAT? HECTOR, DID YOU HEAR THAT? YOU'RE DEAD, HECTOR – DEAD!'

Hector, in fact, did not hear this outburst – not directly. Deep behind the walls of Troy, he was lingering by his family's hearth when messengers came breathlessly and whispered in his ear. He listened to their report without emotion, absorbed in watching his son Astyanax playing about with grown-up battle gear. The greaves made to encase Hector's calf muscles reached above the small boy's waist. Astyanax tried to heave his father's helmet: after struggling to raise it, at last he hoisted the helmet high, and dropped it over his eyes like an enormous bucket, and staggered around with his arms outstretched, crashing into pots and grindstones – before Hector, chuckling, scooped him up to safety.

'Now then, young rascal! I've a job for you. D'you think you're man enough to do it?'

Astyanax, so happy in his father's lap, gave the biggest nod he could muster. Then, in the same secretive way the scouts had relayed news to Hector, Hector confided to his only child.

Listening, Astyanax shot a worried look towards his mother, as if to say: *Why?* – but then nodded solemnly again.

'Good boy,' said Hector. 'Now run and find your wooden sword, and get ready – as we must – you and I both.'

Astyanax scampered off. Hector drew Andromache to his arms. She was quivering, biting her lip.

'What did you tell him?'

'To look after you.' He gripped her shoulders. 'No fretting now,' he added. 'You know I'll be back.'

'*I don't –*' was all she could reply.

Achilles, fully armed, was resplendent to behold. As he stepped up into his chariot he seemed to insult the sunrise with his sheen and burnished strength. The Myrmidons hollered around him, thirsting for blood. Achilles wasted no time. There was a detachment of Trojans which had been bold enough to set up bivouacs outside the city walls. Their sentries had only just reported the distant rattle of his chariot when Achilles descended on the camp, with the darting Myrmidons close behind. There were no overtures to the attack, nor any subterfuge: Achilles simply stormed ahead, not caring if he left his victims dead or groping for aid. Trojan reinforcements streamed out; but no sooner they came through the gates than the Myrmidons harried them across the plain, down to the edge of the nearby River Scamander – where Achilles spread death as if among so many panicked cattle, tipping bodies into the river's soon clogged and crimson flow. A few dazed Trojans made their way back: that was when the message went up to Hector. Achilles, they said, was half-laughing, half-crying while he killed; he kept calling for Hector, only Hector, to save his men from this plight.

So Hector stepped out. Hecuba and Andromache could not bear to watch him go; but old Priam looked down from a high tower, urging hope against fear for his son. Achilles, it was known, had not seen any action for months. He should be out of condition, short of staying power. If once he tired, then – then Hector might have a chance.

Hector reasoned likewise. As he loomed into view, shaking his spear, the Myrmidons scuttled away. The Trojans, too, drew back in awe. For several moments there was a strange hush, as the two illustrious warriors stared at each other with almost fraternal regard. They stood about fifty paces apart. Achilles heard, under his armour, the rapid intake of his own breath. He had not paused in fighting since dawn. His throat was dry. He mouthed a challenge to Hector; but nothing came.

Achilles stepped forward. Instinctively, Hector raised his shield; then relaxed.

'It's a race, Achilles! You catch me – or I catch you!'

With that – to the astonishment of all onlookers – Hector turned, and sprinted away.

Hector had calculated two things correctly. First, that Achilles' pride in his own swiftfooted reputation would compel him to give chase; and second, that in this arena of visibly single combat, Achilles would never send a spear flying from behind. But there was one factor that Hector could not have foreseen. He had started a contest of running in full armour. It was a heavy handicap. Hector's shield alone would have caused an ordinary man problems just to carry it. Fully encumbered, not even Hector could stay at fair speed for very long. Hector presumed that Achilles was under the same impediment. But there lay the magic of Hephaistos: to have crafted a panoply that was all but impenetrable – and yet amazingly light to wield. It was a virtue of design that Achilles had already savoured in his first killing spree. Now Achilles watched calmly as Hector lumbered away. The Myrmidons were screeching for hot pursuit.

'Let's give him a start, my boys,' grinned Achilles. 'He'll need it.'

Then, at an ominously steady pace, Achilles began to follow Hector round the walls of Troy.

Three times they did the circuit. Hector powered along as he had never moved before, with every elastic fibre in his great cladding of muscle straining in the effort to extend the lead. He kept looking back, expecting to see his opponent in trouble. But with every glance, Achilles seemed to be getting very slightly closer. It was like some childish nightmare. The roars from the ground, from the parapets of Troy, from the pounding in his head, began to mingle horribly for Hector. By the third lap, he could sense his legs burning down to uselessness. His head lolled; now he was stumbling. Eventually he tripped and sprawled. Briefly it was bliss to hear his heart pounding upon bedrock. But the roaring outside his helmet got louder. Hector rolled over, raised himself, and blinked. There was his relentless tracker, standing not far away: close enough for conversation.

'Thought I'd wait till you got vertical,' drawled Achilles. 'Take your time.'

Achilles stayed motionless. Hector circled unsteadily, curling his fingers around his spear. He was still panting heavily. Yet he managed to speak. 'Achilles,' he said, 'if – if I kill you'.

Achilles laughed: high-pitched, a cackle.

'If I kill you,' Hector continued, 'I shall honour your corpse. Promise me one thing . . .'

'Go on,' said Achilles.

' . . . you'll do the same for me,' said Hector.

Achilles stared at him. His eyes were wild.

'Y-You don't bargain –' he stuttered. 'You – you *owe* me!' – and with that cast a spear.

Hector lurched aside; the tip struck flinty sparks as it

sheared off nearby stone. Hector seized his moment. Planting feet wide apart, tensing his right arm, he delivered a perfect throw. As he poised and aimed he knew it was good; and sure enough the shaft went straight and swift to its target. No shield would stop its course.

Achilles braced his shield. The spear that Hector had thrown so well hit hard, hit true – and bounced off.

Hector was agog. He looked around. There were no fellow Trojans to be seen: only a restive encroachment of Myrmidons, creeping closer. One of them tossed another spear to Achilles. Hector clutched for his sword; but waved it, as he knew, pointlessly. This time Achilles made sure. Hector folded, retching and hoarsely pleading.

'My wife – mother – home – give them *me* –' he begged.

Achilles pulled out the spear, and jabbed it hard again. 'Feed the crows, Hector. Burial is reserved,' seethed Achilles, 'for my *Patroklos*.'

He raised the dripping spear, and quickly laid Hector bare. Greeks and Myrmidons came crowding around. At first they gaped, to see the body that was there: even in death, Hector was fearsome to behold. But soon they ventured forward with vindictive kicks and stabs. Achilles did not deter them. He was busy with his own agenda. He made a slit in Hector's ankles, behind the tendons. He threaded a cord through these cuts, and called for his chariot. Then he attached the cord to the vehicle, and with a whoop of exultation flicked the reins. His horses pranced, the wheels spun round – and off went the triumphant Achilles, with the lifeless form of Hector jerked and flung in tow.

Odysseus, Agamemnon and the other Greek commanders were discreet observers. Far off, the wailings of Andromache and the other Trojan women could be heard. Huge Ajax sniffed and gulped. He had cheered as lustily as anyone when Hector fell. But he did not like to see this tour of victory. Shaking his head, he retired.

Agamemnon shared the mood. 'This is bad, gentlemen. We must call it to a halt,' he murmured.

Odysseus looked on more impassively. 'No,' he said. 'Let Achilles have his day. He deserves it.'

'I'd like to know,' said Agamemnon, 'how it will end . . .'

'I'll tell you,' said Odysseus. 'Achilles will ride around some more, gleeful with those Myrmidons of his. But he has other pressing business. He must bury his boyfriend – in style. There will be more blood: I believe our hero has a dozen Trojan prisoners waiting to be sacrificed for the occasion. But once Patroklos is laid to rest, then the anger of Achilles will be spent. We shall have delightful games by the tomb, with prizes, feasts and drinking bouts. You, my lord, will be given the seat of honour: Achilles will make peace with you, and you with him. Then old Priam will come in person to beseech for the return of his son's body; and, as you shall witness, Achilles will seem like the very model of goodwill. So Hector's body goes back to Troy. His women scream and shred their cheeks. The end.'

Odysseus paused. He could not resist a final line of prophecy. 'Oh yes. I nearly forgot. And then – of course – the war goes on.'

# TROY TAKEN

It all happened as Odysseus predicted.

Achilles did receive Priam, and seemed the soul of friendliness. Yet he bartered a heavy ransom from the king – to release, after all, a corpse damaged beyond recognition. Priam was not consoled. And as tidings of Hector's death carried beyond Troy, the word also spread that Achilles was now doomed. Warriors came from far away to try their hand at despatching the master of death. One such who came on Priam's behalf was Penthesilea, queen of the Amazons; another was Memnon, a magnificent tribal chief from Ethiopia. Both lost their lives to Achilles. So a contrary rumour started: that Achilles, with his magical armour, could not be killed.

As for Achilles himself: always moody and erratic, his shifts of temperament only became more pronounced after the loss of Patroklos. His first reaction to killing Penthesilea was to burst into tears, lift her up, and deeply kiss her. When Thersites, the resident loudmouth in the Greek camp, cracked some lewd joke about this posthumous embrace, Achilles did not laugh it off. It was the last utterance from Thersites. Achilles flew into a bare-fisted rage that left the poor man pulverized – his brains oozing out of his skull.

Achilles' reign of terror left another mark on the family of Priam. One of Priam's youngest sons was a boy called Troilus, fresh from his teens. Troilus was lithe and winsome, a promising horseman – but disinclined to join the war. His first love, for the girl they called Cressida, had been destroyed by Greeks and Trojans wrangling over her. Now he was careless. During respites from the fighting, he liked to take his thoroughbreds out to canter below the city walls, leading them to a sanctuary of fresh spring water. Achilles, roving alone, sighted the prince, and tenderly declared his devotion. Their liaison was short-lived. Achilles made Troilus promise to return the next day. Troilus, innocently, kept the pledge. He was missing at nightfall. Searchers found him naked and cold by the fountainhead. Beside the body lay a long curved blade: the sort of knife reserved for pious sacrifice.

Achilles made no secret of this. He said he had heard a voice in his head – that Troy would not fall till Troilus was slain.

Grief for unfortunate Troilus did not blind Priam in planning revenge. Beginning to understand Achilles, he sent the bravest of his daughters, Polyxena, to offer herself as a prospective bride to the lonely champion. Trojan delegates took Polyxena to the tent of Achilles, where she was to entertain him for an evening before they escorted her back. Then Polyxena told Priam what she had been able to glean from her intrepid courtship. Yes, she said – she *had* ensured that wine flowed readily into the cup of Achilles. The Greek hero, in return, had spouted like a boastful schoolboy. What had she learned from his bragging? Perhaps not much – only that Achilles had denied the magic of his armour. He asserted he could fight as well completely stripped. He was – he claimed – invulnerable from infancy. He knew that his mother had once dangled him in the death-cold eddies of the River Styx. The only part of him that could be wounded, therefore, was where Thetis had held him fast – by his ankles.

Polyxena's report was taken seriously by Priam. The king

brooded for hours: then summoned yet another of his offspring – Paris.

Since the outset of the siege, Paris had stayed almost invis-
ible within Troy. If he appeared in public, he would only
remind everyone that he was the cause of the general misery.
All he wanted came in the delicious shape of Helen. He hated
to see her beauty imprisoned in this way. He wished the
Greeks would depart; yet he never regretted his love.

Paris came nervously to the royal chamber. It was a shock
to be there. The old man had about him a new fatigue of life;
he seemed to have lost some focus to his sight.

'Paris? Is it my same dear Paris – once the best marksman in
Troy?'

'It is, father.'

Priam's eyes narrowed. His voice hardened. 'Then redeem
yourself, son. Take two arrows. Smear poison on their points.
Station yourself with a clear view to Achilles. Aim for his
heels. You have my blessing. Go. Do it.'

Paris opened his mouth to protest; then thought better of it.
If he succeeded in this commission – and it would not be easy
– there was sparse glory in store. No one rejoiced at sniping –
the dealing of death from a safe distance. But what did he care
for glory? Achilles dead was Achilles dead. If by removing
Achilles he hastened an end to the siege over 'Helen of Troy',
then Paris was sufficiently content. He went away to find his
bow.

Achilles was strutting, at his most defiant – when Paris judged
the moment to fire. Of the Trojans after Hector, by order of
rank and status, Aeneas had been next to meet Achilles in the
field; and Aeneas, being cautious, did not hurry to the duel.
He was trading vocal missiles with Achilles when Achilles
collapsed.

It was, as Paris had foreseen, an inglorious hit. No one, for some while, knew how Achilles had been brought down. The Myrmidons sent up a sudden clamour of grief, yet quickly melted away. As Trojans came forward to pounce on the body, only Ajax offered defence. By instinct he ran to where Achilles lay. With one sweep of his sword he kept predators at bay. Achilles was convulsing, the poison snaking through his limbs. Hoisted over the broad shoulders of Ajax, the hero dribbled a last request – militant to his end:

*'Priam's girl – Polyxena . . . I want her throat slit on my grave . . .'*

It was not the end of the war. It was, however, the beginning of the end.

Immediately the question arose: who should have the heavenly armour of Achilles?

For great-hearted Ajax this was not a topic of debate. He had rescued Achilles in the field. And among the Greeks at large, everyone was agreed: no warrior came closer in courage to Achilles than Ajax. True, Ajax lacked style; but he gave unstinting dependability in all quarters. Surely, then, the arms of Achilles should belong to Ajax.

It was Odysseus who threaded the issue with doubt. He congratulated Ajax on recovering the body. He outlined plans for a splendid burial – nothing but the best. Then he wondered aloud: should Achilles be rightfully interred in battledress? If not – then where should it repose?

Odysseus knew very well that Ajax had his heart set on inheriting the armour Hephaistos had made. But that was merely a matter of manly pride. Odysseus was more concerned with bringing the war to a close. He had probed the oracles – and learned, much to his surprise, that Achilles had a son; and that this son was destined to storm Troy's citadel.

Yet another condition for ending hostilities was also made known to him. Odysseus saw where his duties lay. Ajax and the others would fight till they dropped: they could never see further than the next day's settling of scores. He alone had the sense to cut the loop of hatred that was coiled about Troy. He would do so – but carefully: behind the scenes.

As for the arms of Achilles, Odysseus feigned innocence. It was hard for any *one* to decide to whom they belonged – so what if they *all* shared the choice, and put it to a vote?

'A *vote*?' asked Ajax. 'What's that?'

'Easy,' said Odysseus. 'You give a speech, telling us why the armour should be yours. Then I – or someone else – gets up, and says why the armour should be theirs. Then the listeners say which they prefer.'

'How'd they do that?' Ajax demanded.

Odysseus – not for the first or last time – was thinking on the spot. 'It goes like this,' he explained: 'everyone who's listened has a pebble in his hand. Whoever agrees with *you* puts a pebble on your side. Whoever agrees with *me* – or someone else – puts a pebble down on mine.'

'What size of pebbles?' said Ajax, suspiciously.

'Just pebbles. The pebbles don't mean anything. They could be beans.'

Ajax scratched his head. 'Beans? Why beans? Cooking beans?'

Odysseus sighed. 'All you have to do, Ajax, is state your case. Stand up, and tell us why you deserve to have the arms of Achilles.'

Ajax digested this advice.

'Don't like speaking,' he said.

What followed was a peculiar turn of events. The shining helmet, corselet, greaves and shield were put on general display. The Greek commanders gathered around. First Ajax addressed them: briefly, mumbling and gruff. He told the gathering what it knew: that he, Ajax, had picked up the body of Achilles and brought it safely away from mutilation by the Trojans. He could not think of anything else to say; so he sat down.

Then Odysseus spoke. Here came the turn. He began by saying that naturally the arms of Achilles must go to Ajax. Good Ajax, redoubtable Ajax; no one deserved them more. All present approved. Then Odysseus went on to praise Achilles, and the collective efforts of other Greeks at Troy. He extolled the leaders; but he also paid tribute to the other ranks, to the Myrmidons, and also to those many lowly but necessary fellows who manned the camp – even the late Thersites. The Greeks, Odysseus went on, had sustained their siege of Troy when lesser forces would have lost heart and gone home. Why? Because together they had mustered a thousand ships, years ago at Aulis; and together they would see the conflict to its end.

There was audible assent as Odysseus swelled to his theme. The Greeks had come as an army, not some assortment of heroic performers (*cheers*). No one was taking it easy at Troy; when Hector came down like a mighty tree (*more cheers*), it was as if everyone had pushed. Achilles had died the best way that any man could die: on behalf of his friend. One for another; one for all. And the armour of Achilles shone with that noble legacy: a treasure for every Greek at Troy (*prolonged cheering*).

Only later did Menelaus murmur an aside to his brother Agamemnon: 'Very fine. But – do we know where this handsome bequest will be stored?'

'With Odysseus, I suppose,' said Agamemnon. 'At least – for the time being.'

'Ah.' Menelaus ruminated on this. Then added: 'Poor old Ajax.'

'Ajax,' declared Agamemnon, 'is our best man in the field. The pity is – his barren brain.'

After his very short speech, Ajax had watched proceedings with an interest yielding to bewilderment. He heard Odysseus say that the arms of Achilles should be assigned to Ajax by right. He witnessed how the audience agreed. Odysseus had gone on to say good things about Achilles and everyone else. No problem with that. And then the listeners created two piles of pebbles. One pile was small, the other was large. Odysseus counted the pebbles; and with Ajax still nonplussed, he lifted the armour away.

For several hours Ajax sat alone in his tent. A few of his retainers risked asking if they might fetch him some meat and drink. Ajax accepted a cask of wine. It was nightfall when he came out. He was equipped for combat, and swaying. No one took alarm at the sight. Ajax was so often in his fighting gear, and often enough exhausted by his labours of the day. He was heading towards the pavilion where Agamemnon and the other chiefs usually met for supper and a joint review of the day. Again, there was nothing odd about that – although, as it happened, on this particular evening it had been decided to banquet elsewhere. The entire encampment was peaceful: torchlight, shadows and gentle conversations. Shortly, some Greeks heard a grieving of sheep from paddocks just beyond the palisade, and wondered what was amiss. Those were well-built stock pens, guarding precious beasts: had some wolf got in? The noise got worse. There were panicked cattle, screaming sows. Herdsmen hurried across.

For most of the animals it was too late. Their bodies, marked with crude cuts of butchery, were strewn where they had scrabbled to escape. One sleek pig, blood piping from its side, was squealing in a corner. Ajax stood before it, goading, making lunges. Mutterings, spittle, shot through his teeth.

'*Speak, Odysseus – speak, swine – sword speaks now see –*'

The herdsmen shouted. Ajax spun round. He peered at them; then gazed at the various piles he had made. He stepped hesitantly past the hot recumbent forms, softly prodding some with his weapon's point.

He talked to himself, chuckling. 'Agamemnon. Put up no fight. No fight at all. Diomedes there – you were pathetic. Nestor – no strength left. Stick to pebbles, old man. Menelaus – *Menelaus – pah!* You see, you all . . . see . . .'

Again Ajax ran out of words. He wandered off, shaking his head as if at some very great shame.

The corpse of Ajax was discovered next morning, on a desolate stretch of the shore. He had planted his sword in the sand, and had fallen upon it. A few surrounding palm trees seemed to sag at the sight. But there was little pity from the Greeks. Agamemnon, furious at the loss of livestock, and unnerved by the murderous intentions of Ajax, immediately decreed that Ajax should be left where he lay, to rot on the beach like a fish. Others agreed. Odysseus, however, argued for burial. Ajax, he said, was a decent man, forgivably beset by madness.

'He would have slaughtered us all while we ate!' cried Agamemnon. 'Aren't you appalled by that?'

'I'm more offended,' said Odysseus, 'that he mistook me for a hog. Come. Let us all award him a handful of sand – and move on. We are without Achilles and Ajax, our stalwarts. This war needs cleverness now.'

Researching the future, Odysseus had learned not only that a certain son of Achilles was required for conscription to the Greek cause; but also that one instrument of Troy's fall must be the bow of Herakles. (In earlier times, it was said, Herakles had taken part in another war upon Troy – with his usual success.)

Finding the son of Achilles might prove difficult. Most of the Myrmidons had sailed for home; but a few remained as mercenaries, and Odysseus learned from them that there was a time when Achilles, in his teens, had lived on the island of Skyros. The Myrmidons could not swear to knowing of a son. But they knew that, while on Skyros, their future lord had – yes, had played with girls . . .

It was a start. The bow of Herakles, meanwhile, presented no mystery. Odysseus knew perfectly well where it was. When the Greek forces had gathered at Aulis, their number had originally included a champion archer called Philoctetes – who after the death of Herakles had come to possess the hero's bow and his quiver full of arrows. But while the Greeks were delayed at Aulis, Philoctetes was bitten by a snake. Some said it was residual malice from Hera, because Philoctetes had piously organized the funeral rites of Herakles. In any case, the wound was serious and seemingly incurable. Philoctetes groaned so loud with ceaseless pain that no one could bear it. His howlings were reckoned corrosive of general morale. The Greek fleet had stopped off at Lemnos – the island virtually deserted, years after the Lemnian women had slaughtered their men – and left Philoctetes there to nurse his festering wound.

So Odysseus set off for the islands of Skyros and Lemnos. On Skyros, it did not take him long to locate the boy who must have been spawned by Achilles. Powerful, sharp and terrifying even at just thirteen years of age, the uncontrollable lad they called Neoptolemos, 'New War-Maker', had to be his father's son. His guardians on Skyros were only too relieved to see Neoptolemos taken away – enticed, as he was, by the invitation to assume the armour of Achilles.

The situation on Lemnos was more delicate. Over a decade since his dismal abandonment, Philoctetes was still suffering

– and deeply embittered with the Greeks. He had the bow of Herakles; but it stayed close by his side, and he refused to give it up. Odysseus weighed the options of seizing it by theft or force. But, once again, Odysseus resorted to persuasion. He told Philoctetes that there was just one reason why Agamemnon's task force had so far failed to take Troy: because it lacked Philoctetes. Would the master-archer find it in his heart to forgive – and deliver them? As for the wound, Odysseus promised that there were expert physicians in the vicinity of Troy. He had heard (he lied) that these divine-inspired doctors were specialized in treating snakebites.

So Odysseus brought both Neoptolemos and Philoctetes across to Troy. Neoptolemos soon proved himself in battle: there was in him an indifference to distributing death which appalled older warriors, including those on the Greek side. Philoctetes, too, rose to the occasion. Was it by chance, medicine or divine favour that his old wound healed at last? Odysseus hardly dared to say. What mattered more was that Philoctetes soon felt well enough to go out shooting with his Heraklean bow; and that his first victim was none other than Paris.

Paris died indignantly. After bringing down Achilles, he had found himself respected within Troy – and was called upon to help again on the battlefield. No one had warned him that he might be the target of archery from the other side. Pierced in several places, he was dragged within the walls and laid out for a show of mourning that involved not only Helen, but almost every woman in Troy.

While the city was still distraught, Odysseus made his next move. It began with a peculiar request made to Diomedes – the youngest of the Greek leaders, and the one most sympathetic to his unconventional strategies. Odysseus, dressed in rags, carrying a stick and bundle, asked Diomedes to give him a beating. 'Do it properly,' he instructed, 'though you might save my teeth if you can.'

'And the purpose?' wondered Diomedes, taking the stick that Odysseus provided, and flexing it.

'I'm a slave,' said Odysseus, crouching and bracing himself, '– a slave about to run for it.' Diomedes did as he was told. A little later, authentically decorated with blood-seeping welts, Odysseus limped out of the camp by moonlight. He hobbled across the plain, and presented himself at the gates of Troy as a wretched fugitive. Guards on duty laughed at the sight of him; but the disguise worked. 'Lucky dog!' barked their sergeant, kicking Odysseus as he grovelled along. 'Find yourself a corner, lick your wounds, then report to us first thing in the morning – you can slop out our cesspits.'

Odysseus did not find himself a corner. Instead, he crept and sidled around the city, making a map in his mind. Market square, temples, Priam's palace, army barracks – he saw how all the parts of Troy related to each other; and imagined how they might be destroyed. This was what he had come to survey. Just once he was almost caught in the act. A doorway opened by the palace, and out came two burly soldiers, accompanied by a woman. She was clad in the heavy robes of lamenting – but even in that dull garb she was proudly, arrestingly elegant. Odysseus pretended to be polishing cobblestones as they passed; but could not resist a look at the pale-faced, dark-haired lady. To his dismay, she stared back at him, and stopped: it was a moment of recognition. She seemed about to speak – if one of the men had not given her a rough push and told her to move on. 'You old slut!' they jeered, '– is it beggars you fancy now?' Then Odysseus realized that, with Paris dead, Helen was truly now a captive in Troy. She cast a backwards glance at him; and perhaps, he thought, beseeched him with a quick smile of encouragement.

He must not risk staying much longer. Yet, as he was skulking through the streets – quite deserted at this hour – he noticed that the entrance to the main sanctuary of Athena was ajar. He could not resist peering inside. There, commanding a smoky inner cell, stood Troy's most ancient symbol: the small old-fashioned image of Athena they called the Palladium. Odysseus looked cautiously around. A priest was by the altar: the old fellow yawned, dampened down a brazier, and then trudged away. Odysseus waited; then edged towards the shrine. '*Athena dear*,' he whispered, '*how could Paris have rejected you? Come, now – come with me –*'

He did not so much seize the olive-wood statue as caress it to himself. Odysseus had never felt so nervous in his life: half-expecting the icon to yell, the temple to crash, all Troy to awake at the theft. But nothing happened. He gave the goddess a kiss, and stowed her in his bundle. Then he found a set of stairs that led to the city's upper parapet. If there were sentries assigned to the battlements, they were dozing. Odysseus leaned over and gave a whistle. Soon Diomedes and some helpmates emerged from the shadows below, shouldering a long pole – two ships' masts lashed together. They heaved it up against the city wall, and Odysseus shinned down.

Troy, at last, had been broached.

The disappearance of the Palladium caused mystified distress in the besieged city. But consternation was soon offset by the sight of what was happening over at the Greek camp. Tents were being dismantled or burned. Ships were loading up. It looked as if Agamemnon had finally conceded defeat. Trojan scouts also reported much activity from carpenters at the site. Seemingly they were constructing, from the hulks of some disused vessels, an enormous four-legged effigy. Priam was too feeble to see any of this for himself. But he nodded at what he was told. 'A gift to the gods,' he said. 'They know Aphrodite sways the waves, and she is loyal to us still.'

While files of Greeks embarked, the effigy took shape as a colossal wooden horse. Soon it was all that remained where for so many years the Greeks had kept their station on the coast: a horse, made up of weathered keels and caulked planks.

A few Trojan soldiers advanced to the site, and confirmed it derelict. Then Priam and Hecuba, each frail and supporting the other, were guided down from Troy. They clapped their hands and marvelled at the wooden horse. An inscription was clearly etched on its flanks: TO THE GODS, FOR SAFE PASSAGE: DEDICATED BY THE GREEKS. Priam had guessed as much. Athena's venerable image had been spirited away from Troy; here, miraculously, was its replacement. The king called for ropes, tackle and rollers – so that the horse should be hauled up to sacred precincts within the city.

There were just two voices of dissent. The first came from a daughter of the royal household – Cassandra. Cassandra was the victim of her own strong-mindedness. She was a beauty; and while she was still barely more than a girl, Apollo had become stricken with desire for her. The god promised and delivered to her the gift of prophecy. Cassandra, however, would not yield to him: so, cruelly, he left her with the art of foreseeing the future – but deprived of the power to communicate such insight. Therefore Cassandra could predict – but unconvincingly, since no one believed what she said. Now she banged her fists against the fetlocks of this wooden horse, insisting it must be a trick; but everyone thought she was mad. Hecuba, anguished, asked the guards to carry her off. Cassandra's fury was too painful to endure.

The second warning came from a senior priest called Laocoon. In an effort to appease Cassandra's doubts, Priam summoned Laocoon to perform a rite of purification before the horse was dragged into Troy. Laocoon came grudgingly, bringing with him his two young sons. He cut an austere, muscular figure. Born to the priesthood of Apollo, he had always officiated at the altar according to his own strict sense of what was rightful and good. Asked to bless this extraordinary votive offering, the bearded elder spoke his mind. 'Tell me why,' he roared, 'our sworn enemies should leave such a thing behind? What does it portend? I for one still fear the Greeks – yes, even Greeks bearing gifts.'

With that, Laocoon reached for a spear; and hurled it hard at the side of the horse. There was a splintering as the spear entered timber. But the damage went ignored. The eyes of all onlookers were turned towards the sea. As Laocoon made his declaration, the shallows had started to stir. Now two huge and scaly serpents were rising out of the waves, and lurching rapidly over the strand. There was no doubt where they were slithering. Laocoon clutched for his sons. One sea snake reared in front of him, and tested its fangs on his robes. A tug, and the priest was bare; another, and the boys were too. Both reptiles darted about, hissing hatred at their mortal prey. Then they wove themselves around, and began to squeeze. Laocoon gripped hard and tried to throttle them; but to no avail. Within moments three lifeless forms lay skewed upon the sandy heath. The monsters disappeared.

It was an attack from Apollo – an overdue show of divine spite. Laocoon had, over the years, done little to earn the god's favour. He had defied the normal vows of celibacy, and was openly proud of his two sons. But witnesses to the event were not mindful of that. They presumed Laocoon had been punished for throwing a spear at the wooden horse, spoiling a well-meant act of piety. Efforts were redoubled to bring the horse safely into Troy. The artefact was curiously ponderous to pull; but it was shifted all the same.

The passengers inside the belly of the horse were jolted around – but glad to be on the move. Neoptolemos rubbed his elbow: Laocoon's spear had grazed but not impaled him, and this near miss made the youth even more eager to scatter havoc within Troy. He was describing what he proposed to do with Cassandra – when Odysseus ordered hush. There were about thirty Greeks wedged together there, all armed and ready to fight. But now they must wait till the city went to sleep. Then, as arranged, a beacon would be lit by a renegade Trojan posted beyond the walls: a certain Sinon, whom Odysseus had befriended and bribed. The signal was to be kindled by the tomb of Achilles, on a knoll that could be seen out at sea. For Agamemnon was still in command. He had not sailed off, but simply guided the Greek fleet to discreet moorings along the coast. If all went to plan – this was to be the blazing darkness from which the citizens of Troy should greet no dawn.

Squinting through cracks in the wood, Odysseus judged his moment well. He opened a panel in the undercarriage of the horse, and peered out. There was a full moon above, and the streets below deserted. He took bearings and lowered a rope ladder. As each man clambered down, laden with weapons and incendiary devices, Odysseus told him where to attack. He had special words for Neoptolemos, whose eyes were wild with the mayhem to come.

'Priam's palace is your aim. Leave Cassandra: she's reserved for Agamemnon – with whom your father made a gracious peace. As for the rest – go ahead: let them have it . . .'

Troy's defenders were mostly caught in fires that blazed through their barracks. While the guards at the city's entrance scrambled to the alert that ships had reappeared on Trojan shores, they were attacked from behind; soon the huge gates were smashed from their hinges, a stark invitation to the

Greek forces now streaming across the plain. Odysseus took his place by the same temple he had lately robbed, directing the destruction, and shouting hard – if only to block out the screams rising on all sides. As houses burned, their rooftops came down with cascades of terracotta tiles that sounded like applause. *How strange*, Odysseus thought: *we do so well to live together in cities like this – what satisfaction should any mortal take, in seeing it all come down?*

Already he regretted goading Neoptolemos. Achilles' son was in his element. Pity did not swerve him. Hacking his way through the royal quarters, trailing bodies as he went, the teenage predator at last came upon his promised prize. Priam was trapped in an upper corridor, flailing along in slippers and a nightgown, and holding the hand of his grandson, little Astyanax. Neoptolemos gave a hoot of exultant glee. He knocked the old man down and grabbed Astyanax, holding the child at arm's length by the throat. '*God, no,*' groaned Priam, crawling forward, '*do anything, do what you will, to me –*'

There was an open window to hand, with a sheer steep fall to the rocks below. Neoptolemos extended his reach – and let the wailing toddler drop. Then with his sword he set about the wispy-haired and uncrowned head of Troy's last king.

Hecuba and Andromache and other women of the Trojan court had been pushed into a kitchen below: they would be the servile rewards of war. Now, armed with grinding-stones and ladles, the women tried to fight their way out. They caused injuries; but were in the end held down.

Polyxena was extracted from their number. For all that Neoptolemos had never known his father, he knew of Achilles' dying request. With shrill ecstatic laughter, Neoptolemos bundled his victim out to the cenotaph of Achilles, where just hours earlier the signal for invasion had been lit. The beacon's embers were quenched with particular force: the lifeblood of Polyxena.

Her sister Cassandra sought refuge at the city's altar to Apollo – where once Laocoon had served. A gilded statue of the god stood there: Apollo typically radiant, tall and striding forward, in his grasp a far-shooting bow, his lips curled in remote amusement. Cassandra wrapped herself round his feet. But Apollo did not stir, nor cease to be amused, as she was dealt lewd violence by the first mob of Greeks who found her. When they had done what they would – they tore her away by the hair.

One Trojan warrior resisted: Aeneas, whom few of the Greeks dared attack. And there was the quandary for Aeneas. The intruders not only did not dare but did not *care* to take him on. They had other concerns. For all the years of siege, Troy remained a rich and well-stocked citadel. Many Greeks had designs upon its gold. They were not intending to go home empty-handed.

Aeneas was chasing looters when he heard his name called out – in Greek. He turned: did he have a challenger at last? Perhaps: the call came from Odysseus. But to his dismay, Aeneas saw that Odysseus was in no offensive stance, but came flanked by two figures: one young and one old. Aeneas knew them well. The young one was his son, Ascanius; the other his father, Anchises. The group was joined by Agamemnon, also apparently brandishing no weapon. Yet Aeneas kept up his guard.

'My wife!' he bellowed. 'What have you done with my wife?'

Odysseus spoke calmly. 'Aeneas – we've looked for her. The search goes on. If we find her, she'll come to no harm. I give you my word.'

Still Aeneas was bristling; ready for combat.

'Aeneas,' said Agamemnon, curtly, 'hand over your spear and leave. I'll see you out myself. Troy is gone, Aeneas. You have nothing to fight for now.'

Odysseus, half-absently, tousled the hair of Ascanius beside him. Confined in a sudden island of quiet amid their crashing city, three generations stared at each other. Then a spear hit the ground with a thud; followed by the rattle of an empty helmet. Ascanius dashed forward and leapt into his father's arms. Anchises tottered forward too, but very haltingly. He had taken a bad fall, could hardly walk. He shook his head.

'Damn, damn, *damn*. Look now – I'm useless – a broken crock. Go ahead, go on, you two. I simply can't.'

Aeneas shook *his* head. Still carrying Ascanius, he hoisted his father onto his big shoulders; and set off.

The child asked: 'Daddy, where are we going?'

'I don't know,' replied Aeneas, musing as he descended with his double human load towards the open gates. 'Westwards, I suppose. Across the ocean. We shall start a new city there. Not in my time, nor in yours – but some day, I swear, we shall be back – as masters of this place.'

This promise made the boy Ascanius thoughtful too. 'Will our city be bigger and stronger than Troy?'

'Oh yes,' said Aeneas. 'Our city . . . Well, *our* city will rule the world.'

Father and son were playing a game. But from his undignified position – slung over and humped along like a sack of barley – old Anchises could afford a knowing smile.

Anchises had foresight. He was privy to the future rise of Rome.

From the fall of Troy – one last scene.

In a cellar basement he found her: a lady chained and shivering. It was an unlovely site. But the reunion that happened here was not entirely loveless.

'You took your time,' she said – as a matter of fact.

'Yes,' he said, hammering at the chains. 'It's been a while.'

'I didn't know you cared – so much.'

'No. Nor did I know – till now.'

The manacles fell off. She tossed her dark hair. He slipped a cloak of sable fur over her shoulders. She purred. He gazed on her with some wonder.

'Amazing,' he said. 'You still look . . . like the only daughter of Zeus.'

Then Menelaus took Helen by the hand, and led her away.

# IV

# A HERO'S COMING HOME

# THE TRAVELS OF ODYSSEUS

It would have been a second honeymoon: except there was never a first.

After Troy, Menelaus and Helen were reunited; and neither felt much urgency to make the return to Sparta. As Menelaus reasoned, the kingdom had managed well enough without him for a decade. He could afford to extend his absence – for the sake of rest and recreation after so many years of war. So he and his retrieved wife made a leisurely tour in the east. Princes and pharaohs were glad to offer hospitality to the couple: to hear tales of the battle from grand Menelaus, and see for themselves the unweary truth of Helen's fabled looks. Menelaus had many cartloads of golden loot from Priam's stores; he gave and received many gifts of esteem as he went in stately progress – not only around the coast, through Phoenicia and Cyprus, and down the River Nile; but also in camel trains to Persia, and fabulous lands beyond. Eight years were past before the royal pair came home to simple Sparta, its olive groves and snow-topped hills.

Menelaus had hardly settled in his palace before a stranger was announced. The nervous young man who was shown into the great hall stammered that his father had once been a comrade to the king. He had come, he said, from the island of Ithaca. 'Ah, *Ithaca*,' Menelaus smiled. 'I know who this must be: the only son of Odysseus. Am I right?'

Both Menelaus and Helen were raised on thrones. Around them, half-unpacked, stood their marvellous tribute from far-away lands – sweet-smelling chests of cedarwood, inscribed ostrich eggs, urns of fine-chased gold. The newly bearded visitor was clearly overawed.

'I – he – yes – I am.'

'Your name, your name – let's see if I remember now,' Menelaus mused. '*Telemachus* – that's it?'

Telemachus nodded.

'You see, Telemachus,' Menelaus went on, 'your father was always talking of you. He hated his absence from you. So. What brings you here?'

'*He* does,' said Telemachus. 'At least, I think he does. I mean I hope he does. If he's still–'

'Wait,' said Menelaus. He turned to his queen. 'My dear – should we not entertain this young man – the first guest of our new life?'

Helen slipped away. Moments later, palace staff were shimmering around the chamber, setting out couches, and arranging plump fleeces upon them; bringing bowls of rose petals in cool spring water for tired feet; and filling cups with draughts of beady, resinous wine. Fresh bread came in, spreading its homely aroma; then trays of olives and figs, and platters of grilled meats, flecked with wild herbs.

Helen, barefooted, sat down with her legs tucked beneath her, like a girl. Telemachus could not bear to look at her. 'Don't worry,' she said, gently. 'Eat. Drink. He *is* still alive.'

'Of course he is!' exclaimed Menelaus, through vigorous mouthfuls. 'He's indestructible, that man. But I'd have thought no one would be quicker to get home than Odysseus. It's where he always wanted to be, all through the war.'

Now Telemachus could hardly speak for excitement. 'He's

alive? You know? Where? How far from here?'

'Steady,' said Menelaus. 'Come on – help yourself. You need building up, if you're to be your father's son.' He turned to Helen. 'Where was it, love – that we had the news of Odysseus?'

'Proteus,' said Helen, in her sinuous voice. 'How could you forget?'

'Proteus, Proteus – the Old Man of the Sea. What a tangle that was. We came across him quite by chance, sunning himself on some rocks, along the Cilician coast. You know his reputation? He's a slippery fellow. Slippery as your father – and I mean no disrespect by that. He can change into whatever he fancies: snake, lion, starfish, seal. But I pinned him down, and got him to speak, spitting through all the silvery sprats in his beard. Old Proteus knows all that happens across and below the surface of the briny sea. It was he who told us that Odysseus was alive. Not thriving, I fear – but alive, despite ceaseless tribulations.'

Menelaus paused. A shadow of distress passed across his face. 'Alive is worth a lot,' he added, bitterly. 'It could be much worse. You heard what befell my brother, on *his* return?'

Telemachus nodded.

'*Darling* –' Helen warned.

'We won't talk of that,' said Menelaus. 'It makes me rage too much. Look. We have given you good news, young man. What have you for us?'

'None,' said Telemachus, solemnly. 'None at all.'

As they reclined over never-empty cups, Telemachus shared with his hosts the sorry tale of Ithaca.

For several years after Odysseus departed for Troy, the island was peaceful enough. Odysseus had left his palace in the hands of dependable staff. His own former nurse, Eurykleia, helped Penelope look after the infant prince Telemachus. Until Odysseus returned, the boy's education was to be entrusted to a kindly guardian called Mentor. Laertes, aged father of Odysseus, lived not far away. The palace estates, so carefully laid out by Odysseus, were productive in their yield of crops and herds.

'Too productive, I suppose,' Telemachus sighed. 'Tempting, at any rate, to outsiders. And what with my mother as she was – as she is . . .'

'And how is that?' asked Helen.

'Well – she's my mother, obviously – but even I can see – she's beautiful, and good – almost as beautiful . . .' With a shy glance at Helen, Telemachus blushed, and proceeded to a subject that pained him deeply. 'So, anyway – then these Suitors pitched up. *Nobles*, they call themselves; creeping in from Zakynthos and the other isles around. There's a cohort of them. One's called Antinous. He talks a lot, he eats a lot; I think my mother just hates the sight of him. But another, Eurymachus – well, he wants very badly to marry my mother. He says my father's gone for good, and Ithaca needs a king. He and all the others – they've virtually taken up residence in our palace now. They say they're rich; but if they're so rich, then why are they taxing our farmers, raiding our stores, drinking up my father's wine? They won't leave my mother alone. And they say I'm only a boy, and I don't understand. But I do. That's why I came to you.'

'Do they know you're at Sparta?' asked Menelaus.

Telemachus shrugged. 'Yes. In fact, I think they might have tried to kill me on the way.'

Menelaus lifted an eyebrow. He could detect a junior Odysseus here.

'Your mother . . .' Helen was curious. 'What does she do – to keep all those men out of reach?'

'She has a trick,' Telemachus replied. 'She told them she's busy making a shroud for Laertes – my grandfather. That's true enough. During the day, she stays at her loom, weaving away. Then, at night, she unravels whatever she's done. So it goes on.'

Helen clapped her hands. 'Oh, the clever girl!'

'Yes,' said Telemachus. 'It's worked well – for a while. But the suitors aren't so stupid. They say my father must be dead by now – a pile of bones on a beach. They say it's what he wanted – for her to take another man – if he never came back. And now they've set a date. She has to decide which one of them she'll have: within a week from now.'

Menelaus whistled through his teeth. 'Well,' he said, 'we've told you what we know. What else can we do? But don't despair. Remember, first, that for all that befalls your father, Athena is always on his side. And second, no man is more resourceful than Odysseus. He will be back, Telemachus. Mark my words.'

Even as Menelaus pronounced those words in Sparta, the resourceful man was heading for home – at least, as it would have seemed to an observer from above. Odysseus did not feel so sure. He was clinging to the mast of a raft, pitched to and fro at the ocean's caprice. His clothes had been ripped off his back; his supplies were swept clean away. He had little idea where he was. Sea and gales had all but beaten him. Still he gripped the timbers that survived. Lifted to the peak of a swell, Odysseus had glimpsed dark lines of solid land. He had been punished hard since Troy, and resisted several deaths. He moaned to himself amid the turbulence: could all he had endured be worth no more than such a dismal fate – to be flung onto some tree-fringed beach, lifeless as a log? Had he not been assured of a mellow old age?

Black reefs rose up and caught the raft on their barnacled spurs. Odysseus heard the splintering of planks as they broke on the rock. Now he must release his last support and strike for shore. He tried to swim, but the thick grey waters only mocked his muscle, turning and dragging him as they pleased. Odysseus went under, and his lungs filled bitterly. He chopped about with his hands, and gargled curses as he sank. Then he felt a great surge. A wave hoisted him onto its shoulders and then tossed him along in a bundle of submerged somersaults – onto a stretch of pebbles and sand. The wave rattled back, sucking him along for its sport; but Odysseus dug his fingers into the shale, and hauled himself clear of the foam. He was soon hunched on all fours and retching from his stomach's pit. Yet the sea's thunder was still close. He got to his feet, and staggered towards woodland. Fresh water was all he craved. Swooning, he fell into a trough of dry and musty leaves, and found he could not move. Darkness dropped upon his eyes.

A view from aloft would have revealed that Odysseus was very close to a brightly pulsing spring. As morning arrived on its cool mossy banks, still Odysseus slept in his ditch. What woke him later was not the warmth of the sun, but a distinct ringing in his dreams. It was a sound he had not heard in years: the sweet tinkle of girls laughing.

At once he knew he was alive – and alive, surely, in some inhabited land. Suddenly exultant, Odysseus shook himself free of leaves and stumbled towards the laughter. It came from not far away. The girls were by a waterfall and pool. Some were washing clothes there; others were washing themselves, or simply splashing for fun. Odysseus burst through the bushes. Laughter turned to screams. The girls snatched up their robes and scattered. Then Odysseus realized that he himself was wearing nothing but bruises, scars and a crust of salt on his skin. He tore off a branch and advanced under its frond of decency. Just one girl remained where she was, patiently gathering up discarded garments into a wicker basket.

His voice came from a throat still parched with brine. 'Young lady,' he croaked, 'don't run – just tell me where I am?'

'This is Phaeacia,' came the calm reply. 'Though some will know it as *Corfu*.'

Odysseus fell to his knees. 'Phaeacia, Phaeacia,' he breathed with exquisite relief. 'Excuse me,' he gasped, crawling towards the water. 'No drink – no food – three days –' and he tipped himself into the pool, wincing as the cold washed over the gashes in his flesh, but taking deep draughts as he plunged. He drank and drank, and let the cascade spill upon his scalp and neck. Before he emerged, the girl placed for him, on a boulder, a newly cleaned and sun-dried gown. She busied herself discreetly while he dried. Odysseus put on the gown. It was stitched at the edges with gold.

'This is a fine sort of robe,' he said.

'My father's,' she replied.

'Fit for a king,' Odysseus observed.

'He is,' said the girl, adding: 'But it quite suits you.'

Odysseus bowed to the girl. 'Princess. I could have guessed as much. My name is Odysseus. May I have the honour of yours?'

'Nausicaa.'

'*Nausicaa*? I guess that means you burned your boats. Very wise. I hate boats. Believe me, your ladyship,' Odysseus went on, 'I am not quite the human wreckage that I seem. I should like to greet your father. Will you take me to him?'

'Are you too grand to carry a basket of linen?' the girl enquired. 'Then please – follow me.'

Alcinous, the King of Phaeacia, was a gentle soul. When

retainers informed him that his young daughter Nausicaa had mislaid her entire escort of handmaidens and returned instead with a vagabond whom she had dressed in one of the royal vestments, Alcinous was not alarmed, and let the stranger be brought in. At first sight, it was true, Odysseus looked like a wastrel: his beard gone wild, his face cracked by salt, wind and sun. But once he spoke, there was no doubt: here stood a truly sore-tried man. Could he possibly be the long-gone ruler of Ithaca – the island that, as Alcinous was aware, had suffered sorely by his loss?

Food and wine were brought. For some while Odysseus said little, blocking his mouth with all that his host supplied. Other guests of Alcinous marvelled at the hero's appetite. They marvelled even more once Odysseus was restored, and settled himself on a couch to tell them all how it was that he came to their shores.

'I went to Troy,' Odysseus began, 'against my will.' He spoke in tones of soft reminiscence. He knew he was required to talk; but he was glad, too, simply to gather in his own mind the threads of a life that had lately seemed so close to an end. 'I saw it through; I played my part. It was horrid, of course; though some day, I suppose, there will be poetry stitched throughout the horror of it all. Meanwhile – it does seem very long ago.

'The city was still blazing. But there were others like me – who didn't care to see what happened next. I rallied a crew of those who were eager to go as soon as they could. We commandeered a boat; away we went. We should have been back at our homes within days. With luck . . .'

Odysseus halted. A few of his Phaeacian listeners smiled: they knew well enough when hostilities at Troy had ended. But a cloud of grief passed across the face of Odysseus. He waved his goblet towards Alcinous.

'You, my lord, have an excellent daughter. How old is she –
sixteen?'

King Alcinous nodded.

'I have a son – an excellent son, I would hope. I think he
may be a little older. I can't be sure.' Odysseus stared sadly
into his cup.

'Odysseus – go on,' Alcinous urged. 'Tell us your tale. As it
comes. Then we shall tell you what we know of Ithaca – and
send you safely there.'

Odysseus gathered himself.

'The first people we met, on our way back from Troy,' he
resumed, 'were simply gabblers. You know – the trouser-wear-
ing types. *Baa-baa-baa* is the noise they make; so barbarians
they are. Futile even to ask them for provisions. So we plun-
dered and made off as soon as we could – straight into trou-
blesome winds, driving us to a far more peculiar place. A place
where people live on lotus flowers. Can you imagine that?'

Already his listeners were intrigued. 'Did they gabble too?'
asked one.

'I never heard them speak. They paddled out in little boats
and waved their arms, making signs that we should come
ashore and eat with them. I let a few men go along and try the
purple blooms. Not a good idea. Those men took one taste and
went into instant oblivion. Forgot where they were going; forgot
there was ever a place called Troy, wanted to stay and spend
their lives forever chewing petals. I had to frogmarch them
back to the ships, and shut them in the hold for two days
while they quivered and raved.

'Well – at least we lost no lives in the land of the Lotus-
Eaters. And at least there was *some* hospitality there, useless
though it was. The next isle where we put ashore was a far
more dangerous place – if only I had known. It seemed pleasant
enough from afar. The chink of goatbells in the hills – that's a

promising sound to hungry men. We anchored, and I led everyone a little way inland, up to a cave: huge and stinking though it was, clearly someone's dwelling place. There were cheeses hanging from the roof, and massive pails of milk and whey; a few lambs penned inside, and the ashes of an open fire still warm. We helped ourselves to what was there. I'd brought along some barrels of good strong wine from our hold to offer our host – whoever he might be.

'Whoever, indeed. I guessed he might be big: but when he came back from his pasture-grounds, driving his flocks through the mouth of the cave, he loomed up larger than I feared – he blocked out the light. A shaggy colossus. Then I recognized just what sort of monster we were encountering. In the middle of his head, there was the glowering circle of a single eye. He was a Cyclops – from a tribe of one-eyed giants that have never baked bread, or bothered themselves with the rules of society. I knew at once there'd be no gracious welcome here.

'He shut the cave. He had no door: he just rolled an enormous rock across its entrance. I think he sniffed us straightaway; at any rate, he soon caught sight of us. He asked us what we were doing in his den. I explained that we were on our way home from Troy, spared from death by the will of Zeus, and beseeched this stranger that if he had any respect for the laws of Zeus, we should be treated kindly.

'The Cyclops merely laughed. With one sweep of his hairy arm, he grabbed two of my men, and squeezed them in his fist. Their bodies broke like brushwood in his grasp; their brains bubbled out of their skulls. He stuffed them into his mouth, then reached for a bucket of milk to wash them down. "Nice snack," he said, licking his chops, "– tomorrow, I'll have second helpings of that!" Then he lay down in a pile of straw and fell into contented sleep.

'I know what you're thinking: I had my sword with me. With a few good thrusts into his bulging midriff, I might have finished him off. But then how would we get out of the cave? Not even with all of us pushing could we have shifted that almighty boulder. It blocked our only passage of escape from the Cyclops' rancid hole.

'I lay restless all night, wondering what to do. Some of the men dozed off, which was their misfortune: for when the Cyclops awoke, he seized on two of them, and scoffed them straightaway. I watched him milk the straining ewes, and saw how all of his precious flocks were then ready to be herded outside. He shifted the stone, drove out his animals – then carefully closed the cave behind him, whistling as he went.

'It was time to prepare my plan. In among the muck and straw I'd found a length of wood – some stave our shepherd had left behind: a stick to him, of course, but to us as hefty as a ship's mast. I put some of my crew to trimming this pole, and sharpening one end to a point. I detailed four of them to join me as handlers of the stake, and explained what we were going to attempt. Then I opened up one of the great jars of wine we had brought, and waited for the Cyclops to return.

'He was back by nightfall with his sheep. Before I had chance to address him, the brute snatched two more unfortunates, and devoured them. Still I took one of the hollow gourds he used to scoop up milk, and filled it to the brim with purple wine. "Cyclops," I said, "you don't deserve this. But let me offer you what I have. Here – taste what we brought aboard our ship."

'The simpleton! He curled his hand around the cup, raised it to his lips and tipped it straight back. "Very good!" says he. "What is it?" "A gift from the gods," I replied. "A reward for decent people – those who eat bread, not their fellow-beings." "Give me more," he demanded, "and tell me your name, that

179

I may do something *decent* in exchange."

'My brain was working fast. "Tell me *yours*," I asked, pouring another hearty draught of wine. "I'm famous, I am," he said, with a disgusting great belch. "*Polyphemus* the far-famed is who I am." "Oh, great Polyphemus," I said, "I fear I'm not famous at all. They call me *Nobody*." "Nobody!" he exclaims, taking a third cupful now. "Well, my dear Nobody," he says, half giggling, "here's my gift to you. Because you've been so very kind to me – brought me this delishious boon of yours – I shall eat you last of all." With that he gave a huge guffaw, and fell back, drunk and stupefied.

'No sooner had he collapsed, than I stoked up the fire. When the embers were glowing, I put the end of our stake in the heat. Then it was time to use the tool. We raised the pole, steadied our aim – and plunged it hard where it belonged: straight into the sole eye socket of the snoring giant. The red-hot point sizzled as it struck, and I twisted it in like a drill. The Cyclops emitted a hideous roar, and we all fell back in fright. But the damage was done. He hoicked the log from his eye: with it came a spout of blood and a gush of foul slime. Still roaring, he groped his way to the mouth of his lair, and bellowed into the night.

'We were still crouched deep within the cave. But we heard, from nearby mountainsides, the sound of other Cyclops-giants responding to his cries.

'"Polyphemus!" they called to him. "What's the racket all about? Has someone attacked you there?"

'I couldn't help smiling as I heard the reply that Polyphemus yelled. "*Nobody!*" he hollered, "– *Nobody's attacking me!*"

'There was a silence at this. Then came a few chuckles, and one of his fellow monsters said: "Ah, Polyphemus, you go back to sleep. You'll feel better by dawn."

'Now there was just one more part of my scheme to carry through. As I thought he would, Polyphemus, still groaning with pain, squatted at the entrance to the cave, determined to prevent us slipping out when first light came. But with us in the gloom there crowded his beloved flock – sleek and well-fed specimens they were. Foraging some lengths of twine, I hitched these sheep together in threes, and tied each of my men to the underside of the middle beast. For myself, I picked the woolliest ram there was, and clung beneath its greasy fleece. The silly animals set up a clamour, bleating to get out. Their master knew they had to graze. It was almost pathetic, to hear him crooning to each one of them as they trotted out, telling them not to get stuck in briars or fall into a stream. When it came to my ram, I had to hold on hard while Polyphemus stroked and chatted to his favourite charge. Soon as we were out, of course, I cut the men loose and we sprinted down to the shore. It was a lucky escape.'

Odysseus paused, and held out his cup.

The king himself obliged. 'Luck?' exclaimed Alcinous. 'What else but your quick-turning mind?'

'Perhaps,' Odysseus conceded. 'But then, I admit, I did something very foolish. As we recovered our vessel and put out to sea, we saw Polyphemus quite clearly, stumbling about on the slopes outside his cave. I couldn't resist it: I called out to him – to put him right about my name. "Polyphemus," I shouted, "that was no Nobody, but Odysseus, son of Laertes, who did you harm! I was victorious at Troy; now I shall go home and tell them how I beat you too!"'

'Rash,' said Alcinous, 'but forgivable . . .'

'No. For one thing, Polyphemus in his rage started to pick up rocks, and hurl them in our direction. One hit and we'd have been sunk. Worse than that – the sightless Cyclops prayed to his father for revenge.'

'His father?'

'Poseidon, no less – the Shaker of the Earth.'

'Oh heavens . . .' murmured Alcinous.

'Yes,' said Odysseus, bitterly. 'Poseidon heard – and Poseidon delivered. Need you know more?'

He gazed around the company. The Phaeacians were, to a man, astonished, yet eager for further tales.

'My friends,' Odysseus declared, 'when I am old, and freed from travelling, you *shall* hear what befell me next, and how it came about. It will be woven into verse, no less gloriously than our war at Troy. But for the present, allow a homesick man simply to give you the gist of adventures that I rather loathe, right now, to recall.

'None of my crew survived. That pains me. Most of them were men who stoutly deserved to return. When Poseidon punished me, he also played with them; but each one, in the end, brought an end upon himself. They *would* meddle with their leader's plans . . .

'Leaving the Cyclops to grope and groan by his lair, we came to the Aeolian Isles. Very pleasant they are too, and you must know why: for they are ruled by Aeolus, who is the Keeper of the Winds. Aeolus had it in his power to send us off with a favourable breeze, and so he did. He also gave me a sack, made fast with a silver cord. I had a notion as to what this bag contained, and told my companions to leave it well alone. We began to speed across the Ionian Sea. Confident that Ithaca would soon be within my sight, I allowed myself to relax and sleep. But while I slept, the others grew curious. Wretched inquisitive fools. They were hoping, I suppose, for gold or jewels. They pried into the sack. And out came a rush of opposing gales, hurling us way off course. I ordered all hands to oars, but it was no use: we were blown back, even to the coast of Africa. Dry land was no mercy there. Has anyone,

I wonder, heard of a tribe called the Laestrygonians? No. Then forget you ever did, and don't think of breaching their shores: for they will hunt you for their cooking pot, as they did with some of us. We scrambled away, but then were pitched into a more peculiar place. Another island – which was the home of Circe, who is a daughter of the Sun.

'Again I blame my crew. Imagine it. You have landed in an unknown country. You are sent on a mission to survey the lie of the land. For reconnaissance, I stress, not food. Yet you are beguiled to follow your noses, sniffing the scent of roasting steaks. Pursuing this scent, you are met by a pack of dogs and wolves. These animals do not attack, but rise up on their hind legs, and begin to whine at you. Would you not suspect some sorcery at work? Sure enough, the men I sent were dulled by greed. Pushing past the imploring hounds, they find a cottage in the woods, where a comely long-haired woman stands by a tempting stove. "Come in!" she cries, "you must be hungry chaps!" – and gives them all something to drink. Only one chap has the sense not to sluice down the brew. He bolts back to me as fast as he can. But not before witnessing what happens to his shipmates.'

Odysseus paused, teasing out this twist of his yarn. The Phaeacians craned forward to hear.

Odysseus gave a suggestive snort; a honk through his nose.

'No!' exclaimed Alcinous.

'Oh yes. Like hogs they had behaved, so she turned them into hogs. And spread before them was what they deserved – a trough of slops and rotten nuts. Those whimpering wolves were previous victims of some similar trick.

'Circe was a sorceress. I knew as much from what I was told. What could one do, but pray to the gods for their help? And Hermes answered my prayer. He showed me a plant that made me immune to whatever magic pharmacy Circe might devise. Faithfully, I ate it, bulb and all, as I made my way to her dwelling place. I strode boldly into her kitchen. The devious creature thought she had another mortal for her sport, and plied me with some sort of tinctured wine. I downed it. No snout, no bristles appeared. The antidote had worked. The sorceress was amazed. Soon enough she changed her tone. She started begging me to share her bed.

'Not, I may say' – Odysseus smirked – 'wholly uninviting. But I accepted with conditions. She must transform those pigs to men again. And then put her powers to some use: give us some directions – make the future clear.'

Odysseus lapsed into silence. Again he gazed into his dregs.

'So this Circe – was it she who guided you to our shores?' asked Alcinous.

'If only, dear man, if only. You know where she sent me first? Down into Hades' realm, no less, to seek out the prophet Teiresias. Very cold down there. I shudder to think of it. I saw Achilles amid all the ghosts, and this is what he said: *Better to be a slave who sees the sun than the greatest king in Hades*.'

Odysseus broke off, and waved his goblet at a serving-boy, who hurried over with a jug of ruddy wine. 'Remember that, lad,' said Odysseus to the minion. 'Never – *never* – wish to die.'

The hero took a deep draught from the cup, and seemed briefly refreshed.

'Well, enough of such dark thoughts. Let me tell you the good news I heard from the very lips of Teiresias, the blind man who sees everything, even in Hades' black hole. I am to regain my wife, my son and my throne on Ithaca. True, Poseidon's wrath has tempted me to doubt; and there were many moments, I confess, when I wondered if my visit to the Halls of Death were nothing but a dream. But now I feel the outcome of his foresight to be very close at hand.'

Alcinous drew a mournful breath. 'Good Odysseus,' he sighed, 'prepare yourself for this.' The king glanced around at the Phaeacian nobles for their support. 'You ought to know that in Ithaca . . . how shall I put it –'

Odysseus raised his hand. 'All is not quite how I left it? I know, I know. Teiresias told me as much. There is an ultimate battle ahead. But be assured, I shall prevail – whatever it takes.' With these determined words, Odysseus smiled broadly at his hosts – and yielded at last to an enormous yawn.

'Ah,' said Alcinous, 'and now we are exhausting you. Come, gentlemen. A final toast to our big-hearted guest. I give you – the king of Ithaca: past, present, and future.'

There was, in truth, much else Odysseus might have told. On his return from the Underworld, Circe had primed him with advice on how to steer safely past the Sirens – sweet-trilling seabirds, half-women in shape, whose songs were a lure to certain death. She had warned him, too, of further dangers in the deep: the monstrous threats of Scylla, whose six scaly heads would rear from a rock; and Charybdis, whose waters were a whirling vortex to the ocean floor. Even with Circe's help, these called for all the powers of the hero's nimble spirit and resolve. Then there was the journey to Thrinacia, the radiant pasture-lands where the old Titan Hyperion, father of the Sun and Moon, reared cattle that belonged to the gods alone. The last of the crew had perished thereabouts: having travelled for weeks without meat, they could not resist seizing some of the beasts, and Zeus had blasted them hard for the theft. And then Odysseus was left to drift, clinging to the keel of his shattered boat, until he came to the island of the nymph Calypso. To any other shipwrecked man this might have been a blissful destination. The place was deliciously abundant; Calypso's charms and savours were no less. Yet Odysseus must move on; and there he moped and pined until the lovely but unloved Calypso let him go. That was when he had built himself a raft – and been clobbered one last time by Poseidon's brawny waves.

Those wanderings – that sojourn with Calypso – had taken precious years. One day, as he had pledged to his Phaeacian hosts, all his adventures must be portrayed by bards, and the doings of Odysseus migrate on wings of fame. But now, as he stretched out in the kingly quarters that were assigned to him, the aching wanderer could only harbour thoughts of home. He had been with women of divine and peerless beauty. Calypso had promised him eternity if he would stay with her. But the arms of his consort Penelope were where he wished to lie – and do so in the simple, sturdy bed that he himself had made as the base of a mortal, married life. There was, he proudly reflected, no other bed like it: for its principal post was literally rooted in the grounds of his own estate. He had marked out the tree with care – a grand old olive, unshakable and strong – and whittled it down where it stood. The rest of the tree provided further posts, and a frame; and so a single growth became a couple's bastion.

Odysseus smiled to himself. For all his prowess with weapons of war, he was never happier than when wielding a drill, trueing a line, or chiselling some snug timber joint. And his last thought, before sleep came, was not of monsters rising from the sea, but of a young hound called Brightly, which he had just begun to train before he left for Troy. Was ever a dog so prompt to lick its master's hand, so keen to flush out nests of quail? Had Brightly thrived – and learned to leap at another's command?

Next morning, the Phaeacians were ready to transport their guest to Ithaca in fine majestic style. Alcinous had made available the best ship of his fleet, and loaded it with gifts.

The honoured passenger, however, presented himself as a sorry sight. The freshly laundered clothes that Nausicaa had given him were handed back. Odysseus had reverted to rags. A hideous threadbare cloak hung loose around his neck; his hair was lank; his face bespoke a life of grime. He took gracious leave of Alcinous, and conspicuously limped aboard. 'I'm nothing but a stowaway,' he said. 'You never saw me – right?' With that, he clambered into the cargo hold and settled himself amid some crusty coils of rope. The costume of the down-and-out had served him well enough before: he trusted it again.

So Odysseus landed in the kingdom that was his: a hunched and cringing beggar-man, ejected – with some mock disgust – from a trim Phaeacian merchant vessel as it docked. Once ashore, of course, Odysseus was not acknowledged by anyone. But nor did he, perturbingly, feel very much at home. So many things had changed. Houses were half-built, or toppled with decay. Rubbish sprawled onto the streets. Here was a populace at odds with itself. Some looked as starving as himself; the rest were puffy and smug; everyone abrasive when they spoke, even the children foul-mouthed.

He plodded towards the royal estates. He grew more dismayed. Thistles and quitch-grass sprouted densely in the crops, with other fields untilled. Odysseus remembered great herds of tawny milk-cows, and numerous stock of well-fleeced sheep. Their meadow-lands had turned to scrub where few animals could browse. Angrily he carried on – and then his spirits gained a lift. It was nothing much, perhaps: a shanty-hut upon a knoll, and pigs inside a muddied run. But while the hut was half-collapsed, and the swine looking thin, there Odysseus glimpsed a figure whose sun-burnished features had not altered over almost twenty years: his old herdsman, Eumaeus.

By the hovel a welcome was made – from a fellow unfortunate. Eumaeus was only too glad to share his woes. Odysseus, still unrecognised, squatted in the dirt, and listened amiably.

'There's a word for them what's in the palace now,' grumbled Eumaeus. 'A-feedin' off of someone else's fare. *Para*-somethings – that's what they are. Eatin' an' drinkin' all he had stored, the old master. 'S all disappearin' into their guts, that's where it goes. You won't pick up much down there, not for all the wild tales you can tell.'

'Good sort, was he – the old master?' ventured Odysseus.

'The best,' Eumaeus replied. 'A real gentleman. Laid all this out regular. Me, now – I'd have been nicely set up, I would, if he'd held on. Pensioned off, I dare say, with a proper little house and garden to tend. Anyways – he's long gone. Fact is, he's good as dead by now.'

'Is that the word about?' murmured Odysseus.

'Must be so, eh? Who'd be away so long? The young master now, he would've shaped up right. But now he's gone an' disappeared as well. Didn't want to wait and see his good mother get hitched to one of them para . . .'

'*Parasites*,' said Odysseus, with feeling.

'That's them. Been hanging round a good while now. See for yourself what they've done to the place. All but stripped it bare – and taken my best bacon too. She's no choice now, the lady wife – or widow, as they say. She'll have to take her pick. She should be so lucky, eh?'

'If this lord – *Odysseus*, is that his name?' Odysseus said, slowly, '– *if* this Odysseus *were* to come back, say tomorrow, by surprise . . .'

'And pigs,' Eumaeus hummed, 'had wings . . .'

'You'd be for him, I suppose. What about anyone else?'

Eumaeus shook his head. 'Few of us old hands about now. The cattleman and me. Old mother Eurykleia up at the palace, who gave the master his first milk. Mentor the grey-beard, he's still around – the boy's guardian, he is – but all he lifts is scribing tools. Fine army we'd make, eh?'

'Precious few,' agreed Odysseus, ruminating hard.

Offering to make himself of some use – gathering firewood, hunting for wild salad leaves – Odysseus took shelter with the kind-hearted swineherd. He lost no time in making for the palace gates. All noble households, he told Eumaeus, had food to spare: he would see what he could scrounge. So he saw for himself what had befallen his own great residence. A fine sight it remained, with its throne room and banqueting hall, and many storerooms stacked with jars. But the jars were mostly emptied now. Wine, wheat, oil and beans – here surpluses were kept against hard times, and they should have been replenished every year. Lately, however, nothing but raiding had occurred. And the vagrant Odysseus witnessed why. To take his place as husband of Penelope and master of Ithaca, there was no shortage of volunteers. Dozens of suitors offered themselves, thronging the courtyards day and night. Laws of hospitality required that they be entertained; but they were raucously abusing every kindness they were shown. Not only did they demand the absent master's wine – they stole home with his drinking-cups. Penelope seemed unattainable – so they molested her maids.

It was clear enough who led the chase: a bulbous and officious glutton called Antinous, already striding around and snapping his fingers for service from the palace staff. Close by was a more lean-featured type, Eurymachus. *His* first reaction to seeing a beggar on the premises was to deal a curt but well-aimed kick and tell the tramp to be off. Yet Odysseus stayed true to his disguise. He was inwardly grieved by all that he saw; but who would have guessed as much, from the capers he cut, and his readiness to trade in jokes for any edible scraps?

It was outside the servants' quarters that Odysseus was first recognized. He was foraging there, in a pit of kitchen spoils, for cabbage stalks and less – when he thought he spied an aged and decrepit friend. *So, old pal* – Odysseus mused – *and has it come to this: that we forage together amid a tip?* Could it be? He gave a whistle. 'Brightly – Brightly boy!' he called. Plainly the dog was short of sight, and also very lame. But the mangy tail responded with a feeble flap; and, tottering over to the call, Brightly gave his long-gone master one last devoted lick – and happily died at his feet.

A further reunion came at dawn the following day. Odysseus and Eumaeus were sharing a bowl of barleymeal when a distraught young man arrived. He had made the journey from Sparta by night, because he feared there was a plot to murder him. He was sleepless and scared – but glowing all the same. He had, he said, great news to bring. Eumaeus embraced him gratefully. 'Sit you down, young sir, and tell it to our new friend here: I'm fetching you some sustenance.'

The swineherd hobbled off. Two strangers regarded each other with a curious, searching concern. Odysseus felt his throat go dry, and tears were pricking his eyes. He tried to maintain his part. 'This news you have,' he said, half-choked, '– can anybody share?'

'It's bad for some,' said the young man. 'Or so I hope – that is, if it can possibly be true.'

'Hope no more,' Odysseus grinned. 'My dear *Telemachus.*'

For a moment they stared. Then they fell into each other's clasp, father and son; and there Eumaeus found them, weeping by his humble hearth. The old man too began to sob, barely able to believe how truly he had been duped. Already, to celebrate the return of Telemachus, he had killed the plumpest piglet in his care. So the threesome made an immediate feast, washed down with curdled milk. And while they rejoiced by the dusty shed and sties – Odysseus outlined his plan of attack.

The son found his mother in her rooms. He had indeed promised to be back before long; but that was a promise she had heard so many years before. And so she also held him tenderly. Tenderly, too, she asked what he had learned from the Spartan court. Now it was his turn to act a part. Telemachus gave a shrug. It could be better: it could be worse. Odysseus was not *known* to have perished – not by any report. But neither had anyone, lately, seen him alive.

The time had come, he said, to face the facts. Whether Odysseus were dead, constrained or else flourishing in some distant land, they both knew what his will would be. Ithaca needed government; and now it depended on Penelope alone. She had waited over nineteen years. For so long had she stayed loyal to her husband's name. Odysseus himself would not have wished for her a lonely, ruinous old age. Her admirers were many – which might not always be the case; but now their patience had come to an end. Tomorrow had been fixed as a day of reckoning. There was to be one final feast in the banqueting hall. Then Penelope must show her will – decide among the company.

Penelope listened to her earnest son. If only he had the extra stature and authority that a few more years would bring . . . then she could remain as she was: not daring to hope, nor yet robbed of hope for her husband's return.

But Telemachus had more to say. 'Why don't we,' he proposed, 'do it the old-fashioned way?'

'What's that, dear?'

'A test. A challenge to them all. You know what's in the armoury – my father's hunting bow. It's not been touched since he left – partly because it's so incredibly difficult to bend. We invite any one of them who thinks he can do it: to string and shoot that bow.'

Patient Penelope gave a wan smile. 'Why do you think I've kept those men so long at bay? Because none of them, darling, is the man your father is – or was.'

'Let's just see,' Telemachus insisted. 'Anyway – I fancy trying it myself.'

Penelope agreed. She should not, Telemachus went on, remain present for this trial of strength, but take to the women's quarters of the house – as was only right – and wait for the result. Penelope sadly said she knew what that would be. But she fell in with the scheme. It seemed a harmless game – men, as so often, behaving like boys.

Next day, Telemachus busied himself in preparations for the feast. The two leading Suitors, Antinous and Eurymachus, were impressed. They had been deeply suspicious when Telemachus went off to Sparta, and had connived to have him lost at sea – to get rid of him for good. Now they felt almost ashamed of themselves. The high-minded youth may have eluded their trap; but he had come back full of fresh resolve to settle his father's estate. He seemed positively eager for a final reckoning. Antinous watched approvingly as a few remaining pots of ripe old wine were lugged up from the palace cellars. Telemachus was in the banqueting hall, ensuring where the guests should be placed.

'I've ordered half a dozen full-grown hogs,' said Telemachus, 'and several chines of beef. Oh, and all the partridge to be had. D'you think they'll be enough?'

Antinous rubbed his pudgy hands. 'Should do us well, my boy!'

The walls of the room were hung around with spears and

shields. Telemachus ran a finger over one piece of armour, and pulled a horrified face. '*Tsk!* – just look at the dust on these! Here,' he called to a passing serving-girl, 'we'll have these taken down, and cleaned – they're in a deplorable state. Now, sir,' he said, turning again to Antinous, 'where would it please you to be placed – for this momentous occasion?'

Meanwhile Odysseus too had come down to the palace, and was sidling around the outer walls: if he got the chance, he meant to check the contents of the armoury. But he had not expected almost to collide with his wife as she came out suddenly from a side door, half-hiding her face with a veil. She caused him to stumble. 'Oh!' she cried, helping him back on his feet. 'My fault – I never expect anyone here. Heavens, what a mess you're in – but oh, how rude of me! At least – I see you can't be one of *them*: I mean those well-bred beasts back there. They *won't* leave me alone – that's why I have to sneak out, in secret, like a mouse, as you see –'

Odysseus struggled to contain himself. In the nineteen years since he had seen Penelope, she had grown to graceful womanhood; yet still she had the bloom and twinkle of a girl. His instinct was to sweep her off her feet. But he was plainly a stranger to her – unkempt and shaggy as he was.

'Poor man,' she was saying. 'I suppose you tried for food at the door, and they wouldn't spare you a crumb? Come in with me. Let's see what we can find.'

Bemused, Odysseus followed his shapely wife. She took him into the kitchens, where much baking and roasting was under way, and gave him a plate of honey-cakes, straight from the oven. Then, to his alarm, Penelope called for a bowl of warm water to be fetched – so he could have clean feet. He protested; but it was too late. An elderly crone came bustling up with a basin. Odysseus was horrified. He knew this ancient dame: she was none other than Eurykleia, his childhood nurse.

She had shrunk, it seemed, and her face was like crumpled parchment. But her nanny's manner was as brisk and clucking as ever; nor were her eyes completely dim.

'As if there weren't enough to do, without layabouts at our door,' he heard her muttering, as she knelt and began rubbing his toes with oil. Involuntarily he twitched, and she clawed at his leg with a sharp strong grip. 'Stay still, you rascal; and pull up that disgusting cloak of yours, so I can do this properly.'

The wizened old woman glanced up. Penelope had wandered away. 'A rogue you are, and that's for sure,' she hissed. 'You don't fool me! Since when were starving beggars built like Herakles?'

Suddenly Eurykleia ceased to chide. She was peering at this sturdy beggar's thigh, just above the knee. Her hands began to quiver. What she could see was nothing more than an old scar; but that meant much to her. She knew who owned that mark. It was a wound sustained when he was still an impetuous boy, out hunting boar in forests not far from the palace; she had stitched it up herself. 'Oh, bless us!' she whispered with awe. 'Now what mischief is all this? Don't tell me you're – oh, mercy me!'

Before she reeled back with the shock, Odysseus seized her by the wrist, and hushed her urgently. 'Yes, nanny – yes, yes, yes! But not a squeak to anyone – d'you understand?'

Later, when he was able to speak to her alone, he gave his beloved nurse her special instructions for the night. Once all the suitors were assembled for the feast, let Eurykleia see to it that all exits from the palace were firmly locked. Then she, and all the serving staff, were to do as the mistress of the house – and retire to their rooms.

It was the narrow-eyed Eurymachus who noticed, as the guests began to arrive, an unsightly presence lurking by the door – the same old tramp he'd had to reprimand and kick the other day. 'Thought I told you to get lost,' he menaced, raising his stick.

'That you did!' rejoined the vagrant, chirpily. 'But I have heard,' he added, lowering his voice, 'as how a high and mighty man were going to show himself tonight. And naturally, my lord, I thought – could it be anyone but you?'

Eurymachus could not resist a simper of pride. In his vanity, he had convinced himself that Penelope reserved for him particular regard. Surely she never looked so coyly, so very favourably, upon the slobbering Antinous? At least this craven vermin had the right idea. 'Stick around, if you must,' said Eurymachus, ungraciously. 'So long as you know your station here.'

'Bless you, your honour,' Odysseus replied, 'I know it all too well.'

It was early in the evening when Penelope appeared. Jugs of wine had made their rounds, the hall was packed and rowdy: she caused an instant hush. Never before had she looked quite so stately, yet demure. She wore an expression of grave modesty – yet was exquisitely made up, and dressed for sheer flirtatious power. The assembled suitors lapsed into wonder at the goddess in their midst. While they were still astonished, she spoke to them at large: in a sweet and gentle voice, yet one that filled the room.

'Noble guests. How patient you've all been, with a woman who hardly merited so much of your time and attention. Can you ever forgive the waiting for the sake of one so stricken as myself? But now, at last, I believe I am ready to choose. Before sunrise, someone shall take me as their own: someone present at this feast tonight.'

Odysseus could not be seen: he was crouched, in his rags, just by the threshold of the hall. But he could hear every word, and was shaken by what he heard.

'I have tried to be the best of wives,' Penelope went on. 'If that is a fault, I confess it, and beg you again to forgive. Whoever he is that is destined for me will surely understand. Odysseus rules my heart; and that will never change.

'When Odysseus left for Troy, there was much that he left behind.' Penelope paused; she intended a certain reproof. 'A palace well stocked; and patterns of good husbandry in all the farms and fields around. And among his precious heirlooms, an ancient hunting bow. We have it still, I'm glad to say. Telemachus, dear – will you fetch it? Gentlemen – in memory of my husband, please, I should like to know one thing before I make my choice: if anyone among you here can string and shoot that bow.'

She paused once more, and cast towards every man her supremely treasured glance: a doe-eyed look of mingled hurt, trust and seductive appeal. 'If you love me – will you try?'

A tremor of consternation went round the tables. No one had been warned of this, and no one liked the sound of it; but who could be seen to resist? As Telemachus came back, reverently bearing the massive implement and a quiver full of arrows, Penelope took her leave. No sooner had she gone than voices were raised against Telemachus.

'A fine surprise to spring on us now!' Antinous bemoaned. 'Is this your idea of a joke?'

'When *I* go hunting,' said one suitor haughtily, 'my *valet* strings the bow.'

'Me too!' exclaimed another. 'This simply isn't fair!'

'If that's the kind of party you want,' Eurymachus sneered, 'let's have some other sports' – and with that he picked up a half-chewed bone, and hurled it at the lowly Odysseus. The rafters rang with raucous laughs, as others joined the game. But Telemachus called order. Suddenly he seemed to have grown; his tones were deep and stern.

'You men of rank and dignity, who would be King of Ithaca – what calibre are you?'

He held out the bow, with its dangling cord of wiry gut. At the far end of the hall, a table was uncovered to reveal the target devised by Telemachus: a line of vertical axe-hafts, driven into sockets on the table top.

Antinous felt compelled to reassert his presiding role. 'Well,' he blustered, 'we'll try – of course we will. But only on condition that your mother makes her choice, as she promised – regardless – and that *you* try it too. And – if none of us does it tonight – well then we'll try again tomorrow. After,' he added, 'a proper breakfast.'

Telemachus agreed. So Antinous heaved himself off his couch, and gingerly took up the bow. He tapped it several times, and inspected its meticulously inlaid handle. Then, taking a deep breath, he braced one end against his foot, and pulled on the curved stave.

It might have been made of solid bronze. It hardly yielded at all. Antinous had the string ready and tight between his fingers; but it was still a good way short.

He waddled back to his place. He was an imposing man; he knew this was a futile task. So he shrugged at his sniggering peers, and invited them to prove themselves. For his part, he declared, he had come to enjoy a quaff of wine – not break into a sweat.

Eurymachus was next. He stretched and flexed himself in every way. But the bow was no more pliable to him than it had been to Antinous. And unlike Antinous, Eurymachus took failure with very bad grace. He went purple in the face, cursed savagely, and threw the bow down in rage. As he stamped away, he caught sight of Odysseus by the door.

'What's there to smile about, you maggot? Think you could do any better?' he snarled, and lashed out with another kick. The blow caught Odysseus on the side of the head, and knocked him off his stool. Odysseus rolled over, and gathered himself.

'Funny you should mention it, sir,' he said, haltingly – pretending to be dazed – 'but I think indeed I could.'

This rejoinder brought guffaws from all around the hall. 'Hear that, Telemachus?' someone called out – 'How'd you like to see your mama hitched up with a tramp?' Sensing easy entertainment at this vagabond's expense – and postponement of their own attempts to string the bow – certain young bloods began to pound the tables, urging their host to oblige.

'Well then, old man,' said Telemachus. 'Want to show us your worth?'

Odysseus limped over, to a chorus of jeers, and yet more pelted food. He picked up the bow – and lovingly tested its heft in his hand.

'Just look at him!' there came a call. 'Yes – he's a connoisseur!'

Then Odysseus took his stance. The jeerings faded as he did. That he knew what he was doing was evident enough. His knuckles blanched; the wood succumbed to a creak. It was not effortless – and all the more awesome for that. Slowly the bend in the bow increased, as the muscles of his forearm flexed. One final reluctant curve, and it was there: Odysseus looped the cord onto its notch, and leaned his ear to the taut line. He plucked it once, and then again. *Swist, swist!* was the sound that the bow returned, like a swallow fluting in the twilight air. Odysseus instinctively raised grateful eyes above. And there in the roofbeams of the hall he glimpsed a swallow's jerky tail.

He knew who that must be: Athena, come secretly to observe the scene – and prosper his return.

He took a bronze-tipped arrow and fixed it to the bow. Silence still confounded the room. Then came the quick smart switch of the arrow's release, and a succession of splintering shots. Each of the axe-handles split, as the arrow thudded deep into a wattle wall.

Odysseus straightened up, and shifted his grimy cloak. As Penelope was graced, as Telemachus had grown, so now Odysseus regained the grandeur of his former self. Athena saw to that. His chest filled out, his shoulders swelled. Torchlight gleamed upon his head – and flickered over the suitors' stricken faces.

Odysseus turned to Telemachus. He had one more line of mock-deference to give.

'All these fine gentlemen,' he said, 'have not yet tasted the best part of our feast. Shall we bring it on?'

The company relaxed; but Odysseus fitted another arrow to the bow. He stood where he had cringed, by the entrance to the hall: now he seemed to block it with his bulk. He lifted the bow, and pointed it towards Antinous – who was just, as it happened, reaching forward for a gulp of wine.

'That's it, Antinous!' Odysseus called. 'There's none of that in Hades, that's for sure. One last slurp – before you go!' And again the bow-cord sang.

Antinous had no chance to drink, nor any breath to scream. The shaft went straight through his neck. He slumped. His cup filled with his own hot blood.

Uproar ensued. Tables were shoved across the floor, couches tipped; one of the suitors leapt to bring Odysseus down, and was hit with an arrow that had him pedalling backwards – and fixed him to a wooden post. Telemachus was swiftly at his father's side: Odysseus gave him a nod, and let him slip past.

This doorway was the only open exit from the hall. Several of the suitors had reached for weapons on the walls – but none were there. They grabbed at knives that lay around, and some of them pulled swords; mostly they were scrambling to make barricades, even fighting to hide behind each other. Odysseus pointed his bow again. His eyes were bright with rage.

'Who's next?' he called. 'Who's ready for their taste of Troy?'

Eurymachus had a dagger in one hand. Nervously he held it out and let it drop. He lifted both his arms.

'Odysseus!' he cried. 'You know we never meant you harm. You've killed the man who brought us here. The rest of us – were fools, at worst, who did as we were told. What we've had from your estates, we'll make it up, I swear: double, threefold, what we owe – won't we, lads?' Eurymachus glanced round; then pleaded with Odysseus again. 'Great Odysseus – what d'you say?'

Odysseus stared at him, unmoved. 'I *say*,' he said, '– you don't.'

With that he levelled his sturdy bow. The arrow's force brought a gasp from Eurymachus, and flipped him into the air. Writhing, with crimson running from his lips, he grimaced around the room.

*'Get him, all of you . . . cut him down!'*

The others rallied and charged. But even as they did, Odysseus stepped aside. And in rushed Telemachus, decked in armour and bristling with spears; and behind him, old Eumaeus, and the loyal cattle-hand: both with helmets lodged over their brows, each jabbing a pitchfork as he advanced. Odysseus took a heavy sword, and met the suitors' assault. With one swipe he laid several to the ground; as he moved among the rest, his helpmates added deathly thrusts.

The battle soon dissolved. It was Telemachus, breathless,

who had to hold his father back. Odysseus, and perhaps his trusty stockmen too, might have pursued the slaughter to its end. But sufficient bodies had leaked their lifeblood on the flagstones of the floor. Telemachus was wise enough to sense when justice had been done. For all their arrogance and greed, the suitors of Penelope yet belonged to families within or near the bounds of Ithaca. Trapped in corners of the hall, they were squirming for mercy – mercy that might be quickly shown, and long recalled. So Odysseus, sweating and exultant in the kill, was steered to lower his sword. His arms were dripping blood, he twitched to finish the purge; but Telemachus held him close, until their hearts were calm.

'Home,' whispered Telemachus. 'You have your home.'

The last stars were fading when Odysseus went to his wife. He had been fondly, thoroughly scrubbed and polished by his former nurse. He was shining all over; his hair tumbled round his shoulders like hyacinth blossom.

At first he was dismayed. She shrank at his approach; could hardly bear to look at him. Then he remembered what it was that he and Penelope knew, and they alone in the world. Without a word, he led the way. They passed into the marriage chamber: she had not slept there since he departed for Troy. Odysseus drew back the covers of the bed, and knelt down by its wooden frame. All four posts were finely turned, but he knew which one it was: the single olive pillar that was rooted where it stood. He shook it gently. It was firm.

'Now that,' he said with pride, 'is what *I* call a crafty piece of work.'

And that was when she flung herself on him.

# V

# THE STUFF OF TRAGEDY

# THE HOUSE OF ATREUS

*Well-walled Mycenae* ... That is how Mycenae was, and how it yet appears: encircled by a hug of compact masonry. Who stacked those massive, many-sided blocks, all so meticulous and neat? It looks as if some errant Cyclops amused himself at the site – choosing boulders from a pile, trying every one for size. A fortress built as if to outdo Time – or else to say, *What happened here remains.*

A pair of lions may be seen, carved in local stone. Both stand rampant on their paws, above the entrance gate – an emblem of the place. Agamemnon's citadel: welcome – but beware. The walls you see are fringed with asphodels; a settlement in ruins now, trickling over a sunlit hill. But the record of what happened here is not pleasant to inscribe. The contents of Mycenae are a genealogy of doom.

The beginnings, however, lie elsewhere: upon an Asian peak called Sipylos. It rises above old Smyrna, in the Lydian lands where Tantalos once ruled.

Tantalos was an offspring of Zeus, and keeper of a kingdom that was rich enough; yet Tantalos was not himself a god. Perhaps he resented that fact. Or perhaps he tried too hard to win himself some measure of divine approval. Whatever his motives might have been, Tantalos did not do well when, one evening, he hosted a feast on the summit of Sipylos to which he invited the gods. His guests brought nectar and ambrosia and other indescribable delicacies. Then Tantalos served the stew he had made. He was aware that the Olympian deities were saluted as 'all-knowing'. Let him test their taste buds. Would they know what it was that Tantalos offered: tender pieces of Pelops – the king's own son?

They would indeed; though not before one of them, Demeter, had gnawed her way through a shoulder blade. Throwing the joints back into a cauldron, Rhea, the mother of Zeus, quickly reassembled the boy Pelops. She made good the missing scapula, replacing it with one of ivory. As for Tantalos – he was punished by Zeus. He was consigned to the Underworld to be forever teased – *tantalized* – by water he cannot quite stoop to drink, and food he cannot quite reach to eat. As for Pelops, some amends were made for the butchery at his father's hands. Pelops seemed not only repaired but reborn. His winning looks immediately made him a favourite of the god Poseidon, who gave him some splendid young colts, as well as chariot-riding skills.

On gaining manhood, Pelops set out to travel. He went deep into the land to which he would later give his name – the Peloponnese, or 'Isle of Pelops'. There he found the woman whom he wished to make his wife.

Her name was Hippodameia, which means 'Subduer of Horses': she could match any man in riding or running. She was a princess, the daughter of King Oinomaos. This Oinomaos ruled the western margins of Arcadia, in whose forested glens people lived carefree on acorns, honey and milk. But Oinomaos was a dark and difficult man. 'Heavy drinker' is what his name implies. There were rumours that his wife was also his mother; rumours, also, that he loved his daughter Hippodameia too lovingly. Oinomaos had been warned by some oracle that whoever married Hippodameia would be the cause of his death. He did not intend to let her go. Any man who wanted to take Hippodameia must first prove himself in challenge with the king.

The contest was a chariot race starting out from the royal city of Pisa, by the sanctuary of Zeus at Olympia, and ending at the altar of Poseidon on the distant Isthmus of Corinth. But this race had a history of not reaching the finish. The suitor was allowed to set off first, accompanied by his would-be bride; then Oinomaos gave chase. One overriding rule applied. If the king caught up with the suitor, it was his right to despatch the boy with a spear-stab to the back.

Pelops, granted fine horses and chariot-handling prowess, had reason to hope for the best. King Oinomaos, however, possessed a team of magical and unbeatable steeds. When young Pelops arrived to make his bid for the princess, a dozen or so young men had already perished in the same attempt. The king kept stark victory trophies: a set of grinning skulls, arranged above the lintel of his door. Pelops wavered at the sight: what could he do but pray to Poseidon for extra speed? Yet as he burned for Hippodameia, she burned for him. Eros welded them with recklessness. And Hippodameia had an idea. Her father Oinomaos liked making a show of his own experience at handling the reins. But the royal chariot was maintained by its regular driver, called Myrtilos. Hippodameia went secretly to Myrtilos while he prepared the machine for the race. She found him testing the chariot's twin wheels – secured to its axle by two stout cotter pins of bronze. Hippodameia suggested to Myrtilos that he take out one of these metal pins and substitute it with a replica in wax.

Why – Myrtilos wondered slyly – might he want to scheme against his master? When Hippodameia replied 'For my sake', she may not have intended what Myrtilos understood. All that mattered to her was that Pelops did not join the nodding balustrade of losers' heads.

Hippodameia stood by Pelops while the race was mustered. While Pelops set off with her, the king put a ram to sacrifice. Then he clambered aboard, shaking the reins in one hand and a spear in the other. Now for the challenger's come-uppance. Oinomaos was gaining hard on Pelops – when his chariot lost a wheel and slewed off its course.

It was a perfect accident. King Oinomaos was thrown, dragged and trampled to death.

Pelops was left with double guilt. Though no one much regretted it, there was the death of Oinomaos. Then there was the bargain with Myrtilos. Myrtilos came with Pelops on a journey of purification to the sea. The charioteer grew insistent that Hippodameia had promised him her favours. The two men fought; Pelops hurled Myrtilos into the deep. As Myrtilos went under, he gurgled a curse. He called for doom to fall upon the descendants of Pelops and Hippodameia.

Doom is a weight. Doom obeys its gravity.

Pelops had two sons. Atreus and Thyestes were their names, and they quarrelled all their lives – as Myrtilos would have wished. Both coveted a kingdom that lay beyond the Arcadian hills. It occupied a rocky hump, where Perseus of old had alighted on his way, established as a citadel – not far north from Tiryns, where once Eurystheus ruled, the same Eurystheus whom Herakles had served. This was Mycenae, the city of mighty fortifications. Mycenae went to Atreus.

Atreus exulted in his prize. The slopes around Mycenae were already browsed by healthy flocks. He promised thanks to Artemis for that: unstinting sacrifice. But when the tithes were due, his mistrustful nature made Atreus hold back. He kept the best ewes for himself – as Artemis observed. For the time being, however, the goddess reserved her wrath. She would straighten the ways of Atreus when it suited her. Meanwhile, the siblings' rivalry thrived.

Thyestes was put out. He schemed to make himself chief of Mycenae. He seduced his brother's wife, was banished and returned; and so the quarrelling went on. The pair were set on trumping cruelties – and none more spiteful than a rare communal meal. Proposing that they seal a peace, Atreus invited Thyestes to a supper he had cooked himself. It was a hearty stew – grotesquely so. The ingredients were tenderlings: the children of Thyestes. And the guest devoured them all before he knew what he had done.

Thyestes was to raise a further son. Aegisthus was his name: raised in secrecy, this offspring was primed to gain revenge on any of the breed of Atreus. Two sons, meanwhile, were left by Atreus. The first born was Agamemnon, heir to Mycenae's throne. The younger took himself elsewhere in Pelops' Isle. That was Menelaus, who established Sparta as his realm.

Agamemnon gloried in his kingly role. At Mycenae he loved what went with eminence: the cups and masks of beaten gold, the massive leathern shields; helmets built of boars' tusks, big-pommelled swords, knives with inlaid hilts. He rode around in a chariot of gold; he built domed vaults for the trappings he amassed. He extended his dominion, too – over plains of dependable pasturage, with herds of chargers branded as his own, claiming Argos and its hinterland. Broad-shouldered Agamemnon, lord of matchless wealth – such was the reputation he enjoyed. So when the Trojan crisis came about, all eyes (he felt) were looking to him. Abduction of his brother's queen, and by some upstart foreigner – it was an insult to the family, and must be punished hard.

For Agamemnon, much honour was involved in this. Not

so much in Helen's return: although she was the sister of his own wife Clytemnestra, Helen was dispensable. The lure was the place where Helen had gone: the faraway stronghold of Troy. Mycenae was reputed for its stalwart walls. Troy was better known, as *Priam's city, rich in gold*. Agamemnon wanted it. Gold gathered in his head. What king could have enough?

So it was not the face of Helen that launched a thousand ships. It was proud Agamemnon who marshalled the confederacy. Never had such a fleet been set to sail. But, for day after day, set to sail it was: stranded without a breeze, idle in the shallows of Aulis, waiting to depart. What if its admiral had declared: 'This is a sign from the gods – that we were never meant to leave. Now let us all go home.'

*What if, what if?* . . . There goes tragedy's refrain.

Allegations told that Agamemnon, so leonine to behold, had boasted of his skill at hunting stags – favoured beasts of Artemis. The goddess had not forgotten her neglect by his father Atreus. She descended on Agamemnon, determined that he learn his place. She stopped the winds. The expedition's priest conveyed what the goddess ordained. As ever, Artemis demanded blood – the blood of Agamemnon's young.

Agamemnon had three children by Clytemnestra. They were Orestes, Electra and Iphigeneia. Iphigeneia, a sweet-natured girl, was the one who had come to bid farewell to the army on its way. Already Agamemnon was planning how to use her before the force embarked. An ally had appeared who looked unusually formidable – and who might be in need of a wife. Iphigeneia and Achilles: he liked the sound of that. Then came the calm. Achilles and the other Greeks soon got bored; the whole enterprise seemed about to dissolve. The marriage bond was not to be. Instead, he had a penalty to pay.

Agamemnon was anxious to do as piety required. He was

also determined not to lose face. Accordingly, he had his daughter bound and brought to the altar. He got as far as raising the knife.

At the final moment, Iphigeneia was spared – but not by any second thoughts from the man about to slit her throat. A breeze sprang up, the mainsails flapped: great Agamemnon's mission was on its way at last. The leader resumed his command. That lifting of the blade – he laughed it off, it was a stunt; she'd proved herself a worthy girl, and Agamemnon's own. The victim was less convinced.

Iphigeneia was transformed. She became a votary of Artemis, serving the goddess in Tauris, a remote stretch of steppe-land on the shores of the Black Sea, where warrior tribes subsist on blood and carve their cups from enemy skulls. Bleak as that territory was, Iphigeneia stayed. Loyal to her chosen cult, she never returned home. But tales of the sacrifice episode made it there; as did sundry news from Troy.

Back inside Mycenae's walls, Clytemnestra stored these tidings in her heart. What occurred on the altar at Aulis had been enough: she could not begin to measure how deeply she hated Agamemnon then, with all it proved about his trammelled, blundering, murderous pride. Then followed the more predictable reports throughout the siege of Troy: his petty conquests and his concubines. Years did not abate the rage she saved for him. Each night of Agamemnon's absence, she uttered a heartfelt prayer: that deep within her husband's guts, a Trojan spear might find its home.

Must she only wait and pray? Not quite. When they brought her news of the dispute between Agamemnon and Achilles – which lofty lord should have possession of some local girl – Clytemnestra laughed aloud. For now she had a lover of her own. Not that she had sought one out. This man, a stranger, had come to her. She grew fond of him. He was a quiet, unobtrusive sort, who shared her woes – and something more besides. He listened to her bouts of hatred carefully. She swore she wished for nothing less than Agamemnon dead. He said he understood. Her wish, he said, was his command.

A kindly, humble and supportive man. Such was Clytemnestra's concubine, Aegisthus.

The rest shakes out, as tragedy will. Puffed up with eventual victory, Agamemnon swaggered back. He brought war-spoils in his train; and, among the golden haul from Troy, some living salvage too: Princess Cassandra, rescued from the ruins – a piece of Priam's royal line. Cassandra was splendid to Agamemnon's eyes – except when she began to frown, and claim to have the gift of second sight. Then she only made him laugh, with her fantastic dreams of what might be. Mycenae's first lady – sleeping with an unknown cousin of the king? A giant spider's web, in which the king must die? Axes flying, glinting with blood? He chuckled at the thought of it, and reassured the girl. These were, he said, the nightmares of a soul too long besieged. Not to worry any more: all of that was left behind.

Cassandra half-believed him, as they sailed into sight of Agamemnon's domain, and the Trojan contingent came ashore. King Agamemnon's jewelled chariot was waiting for him there, to take him home in triumph. Heralds went ahead. Bonfires seethed on the hills. From Argos to Mycenae there were hymns of welcome, spit-roasts at every local shrine, and dancing along the way. It could not have been a more rapturous return, and Agamemnon revelled once more in his local majesty. At last the procession reached Mycenae, and passed beneath the Lion Gate. Here even Agamemnon was amazed. A purple carpet stretched before him, throughout the winding city streets. He wondered whether he should step on it: was this not rather fitting for a god? Clytemnestra urged him on. Because he had done mighty, terrible things, she said, this was the honour he was due, and to him alone. Let him proceed, and go up to the royal house of Atreus. What awaited him there was the banquet of his life.

It was a trap, as Cassandra had foreseen. A net dropped on the king as he reoccupied his couch. His wife had woven it herself. Entangled, and without his retinue, there was little he could do. So Agamemnon, veteran of battle, was easily despatched – by one delicate man with a sword, and a furious woman wielding an axe.

Cassandra, too, did not survive: no place for her, in Mycenae's new regime.

And yet the family reunion was not quite complete. Iphigeneia had exiled herself. But two other children were coming of age: Orestes and Electra. Both had been lodged with guardians when their father returned and met his end. Both had scarcely known the man; if they had, as Clytemnestra told herself, they should feel grateful to be deprived of such a brute. But neither loved Aegisthus at their mother's side; and he, in his turn, detested them too. There was a depth of mutual loathing that puzzled the trio; it seemed to come from far beyond the three of them. Orestes carried the burden of some vague and dutiful need to settle scores. Electra fretted in a more particular way. She took to standing close by Agamemnon's tomb, and muttering to his spirit there. She probed the manner of his death; sought out his comrades of old, researched his virtues as a king, and brooded on her loss. She fed Orestes with her cause. Orestes must carry it out. Ignore, if he could, their father's untimely demise. What had Aegisthus done except waylay and slay Mycenae's head of state? If Agamemnon was no more, Orestes was the next in line – and should be on the throne.

Orestes trekked to Delphi, and sought Apollo's word. Calm Apollo, by himself, might have called the misery to a close. Not so his sister Artemis. The house of Atreus, she said, still had outstanding debts of blood to pay. So Orestes was charged with furthering the feud. Electra was glad and keen; her brother less convinced. Destroy Aegisthus, yes. But Aegisthus would not go alone. Orestes saw it clear enough. Mycenae's ruler was the queen. Aegisthus only did as Clytemnestra instructed; her wish was his command . . .

Orestes did as *he* was told – by Apollo's oracle, and Electra's ceaseless challenging. It happened as he feared it would. He put Aegisthus to the sword; and Clytemnestra tried to be her lover's shield. Then he was left with no one to hate – but himself.

Orestes fled from the scene. Yet torment did not let him go. He bore the blood-guilt in his dreams; was harried by spectres and shrieks. Call them Erinyes, or 'Furies', perhaps; they may also be Eumenides, 'the Kindly Ones' who in the end placate all evil deeds. Nonetheless, Orestes murdered his mother: that would be his fame.

Electra mourned through spinsterhood. Orestes died in a remote land.

Mycenae crumbled, save its walls. Of the noble house of Atreus, all that remained was bones. The bones were laid in graves with swords and gold, from which they seemed inseparable.

# OEDIPUS

Some say a threshing floor is where it all began – the action we call 'tragedy'. That may be true. Bread-eating people need to thresh – to whack their sheaves of wheat about, shaking grain from husk and chaff. And long ago, it seems, they did this flailing in a ring, or stamping ground – a rustic orchestra. To dance, to sing, to hope for food; to thank the gods for good returns, and gather stores against the winter's cold: these harvesters rehearsed the drama of collapse. They made a spectacle of ruin. They acted out the worst of times.

And so it goes, the tragic mode. Imagine death. Create wreckage and waste, play havoc. Appear to break taboo and rules. Pretend total loss; cavort in a pantomime of misery. Does that feel good – to try it out, inside the threshing circle, everything going awry? Of course it does. We watch what we abominate. We are not killed. We pity and we cry.

Demeter ripens what we plant, from seed to bearded stalk. But when we cut and bind the crop, another god presides. Dionysos is there, benign and dangerous. He was cradled in a winnowing-fan. Of all the Olympian deities, only Dionysos knows what it is – to be tossed and torn apart. As he recovered: so shall we.

Fellow bread-eaters, huddle around. Here is a theme of vintage revelry: the dark sorrows that beset the line of ancient Thebes.

Cadmus came to Greece from Tyre, a city on the coast below the cedar-bearing heights of Lebanon. He came in search of his sister, Europa. She had been brought away from Asia by Zeus, borne on the back of a galloping bull. Europa settled on Crete, but Cadmus never found her there. Without the missing princess, he was forbidden to return. So he wandered on. His progress took him beyond Athens, and into the plains of Boeotia. This region suited him. He sowed a city by a spring, and called the city Thebes.

All Cadmus brought with him was carried in his head. It was a set of signs for things. In his Phoenician homeland, such signs had long been in use. In Greece they were a novelty. Before the arrival of Cadmus, a cow was just a cow. Cadmus showed the natives what his signs could do: how many cows could be goaded onto blocks of wood or stone or clay. *Alpha, beta* – so it went, this trail of mutterings, until at last came *omega*. Cadmus shared his secrets out, yet used them cleverly. If cows could live in scribbled fields, those cows belonged to him.

Thebes flourished; Cadmus too. He married Aphrodite's daughter, a girl called Harmonia. But harmony was not ingrained among their brood. Bad happenings occurred at Thebes, and some were sheer bad luck. To cite the grandson, Actaeon: was it any fault of his, to go roaming through a forest with a pack of hunting hounds – then stumble upon a gladed pool, and glimpse a white-skinned woman bathing there? He was not out to spy on her; nor, having seen her, did he feast his eyes. How was he to know that she was Artemis?

Actaeon knew instantly. The goddess dowsed him in the scent of prey: his own dogs ripped him apart.

One of the daughters of Cadmus was Semele. Hers was a fate that we have come across before. She attracted the fancy of Zeus, and therefore Hera's jealousy. Hera had grown wise to the art of reprisal, and acted cleverly. She expended no rancour on Zeus; and appeared to Semele as a friend, without a hint of blame. 'My dear,' she said, in a confidential way, 'what an honour for a maiden such as you. But listen: don't let him come to you in any strange disguise. What girl wants loving from some noisy swan or great big heaving bull? Demand of Zeus to see him in his element divine.'

Hera soothed Semele's doubts. 'He'll be reluctant, I expect. Men always are; they hate revealing themselves. So make a bargain with him first. Say you'll love him only if he gives you anything you want. Let Zeus agree to that. Then you insist: you want him *as he is.*'

Semele made the pact with Zeus. He promised he would grant whatever she desired. She made her wish. When Zeus heard what it was, he sadly shook his head. *No, no,* he said. *That wouldn't do at all.* So, asked Semele – was it true: the all-powerful god was afraid of revealing himself? *Afraid for you,* he replied. *Do* it for me, Semele insisted. *You're absolutely sure?* said Zeus. She was.

And so Semele was struck – with gongs of thunder in her ears, by love and lightning at once. She shattered in the blast. There was little left of her. What little there was proved precious enough: a foetus, which the fire of Zeus immortalized. Zeus scooped up the nodule himself, and inserted it into his thigh. In time it emerged as a miniature god – the tiny Dionysos.

Hera sparked with jealousy. Recruiting Titans for the task, she had the infant seized and ruptured limb from limb. But Dionysos was fated to defy destruction of all sorts. Zeus called on his mother, Rhea, to reassemble the babe. Then he entrusted it to Hermes. Hermes teased the child – dangling before it a bunch of grapes – then took young Dionysos far away from Hera's glinting eyes: to be nursed on a mountain called Nysa, deep in Asian lands.

Dionysos passed his early years in women's company. (That is why, though bearded and tall, he wafts about in flowing robes.) Once grown, he made a pageant of his Olympian return. He knew he was unbreakable. He was exuberant and lax; he scorned solemnity. As he had gained immortal status by hazard, so this outsider-god was easy with his grace. Anyone could follow him, however humble they might be. Anyone – and anything.

The train of Dionysos was a riot on the move. Bulls and rams pulled it along, but other creatures too: ponderous grey elephants, and panthers in harness. Slaves hastened to the entourage; wives ran away from their spindles and looms. Dionysos welcomed them. He gave them new identities. The men he offered horsey parts – a tail, some hooves, perhaps a phallus too. They were his satyrs: fat and padded for falling about, devoted to mischief and fun. The women he told to kick off their shoes. Bacchantes they became, or maenads – 'maddened ones' – possessed by the god. They unbraided their hair and let their gowns hang loose. They draped themselves in mottled skins, or furs from any animal they caught. Frenzy made them fearless. Live snakes served as jewellery. Their weapons were bare hands; their banners giant hogweed stems, tricked out with ivy or vine.

Vine-tendrils spread wherever Dionysos took his boisterous band. Vines made a garland of release, escape and ecstasy. Dionysos knew what to do with the fruit: stamp the grapes; ferment the juice. The result both fortifies and fuddles us, and that is as he wished. Since we are born to dissolve, we may as well moisten our being while alive.

Dionysos saw how mortals occupy the earth without any claim to bliss. So he sanctioned tragedy. We may bring disaster upon ourselves; or disaster may clout us whatever we do. We drink and dance while we can, if only to forget the fact: that tragedy is ours to keep.

Then raise a cup, and take a front-row seat: to Thebes again, for tragedy's perpetual and loud *encore*.

Some generations after Cadmus ruled, Laius was enthroned. King Laius chose a youthful queen, Jocasta; with hopes, in time, to raise a family. But on his wedding night, Laius was taken to one side by an ancient resident of Thebes, the blind seer Teiresias. No one knew how old Teiresias might be. He was wise to all that occupied the past, and claimed to glimpse with inner eyes whatever the future held. Now the prophet warned Laius sternly to beget no heir – if he cared for his life.

Teiresias brimmed with advice. Young Laius listened dutifully – but not for very long. What use was it to be a king, if he could never impose his will? Soon Laius quarrelled with Teiresias, and had him expelled from Thebes. Meanwhile Jocasta yearned to bear a child. Her husband seemed nervous in bed; she knew how to deal with that. One night she caressed him with wine. His worries drowned; she gained her pregnancy.

The couple did as many others would: they sought Apollo's oracle on prospects for the birth. But Teiresias had been right. The Delphic response was not what they wanted to hear. A son indeed was predicted, healthy and strong at birth. But the good news finished there. This bonny boy was loaded with doom. He was destined for two terrible ends: first, to cause his father's death – and then to share his mother's bed.

Laius blamed Jocasta, of course, and resolved to destroy their boy. But no sooner had the babe been born than he balked at doing it himself. It was hard to believe that such a placid bundle could wreak upon them any harm. And – as Jocasta pointed out to him – while it was wise to heed Apollo's warning, yet it was no less a crime, to kill this child of theirs. So they entrusted the bundle to a shepherd belonging to Thebes, with orders to take it up to a mountainside – to be exposed and to die. Laius, haunted by the fear that it might somehow crawl to safety, maimed the infant – driving a nail through its heels. That would immobilize the wretched thing.

But shepherds are not the destroying sort. Their call is to preserve – to care for living things. And, by the nature of their work, they keep their own domain: a myriad of paths and drovers' tracks that thread through screes and peaks. One shepherd took the package up, to the heights of Mount Kithairon – but could not bear to leave it there. He removed the pinion through the heels, and passed the infant to a pair of friendly hands, wishing that it be spirited far from Thebes; and so to other shepherds all along the way. The boy was suckled by their ewes, and so survived – until one day he was brought down from the high pastures, as a curious gift to the King of Corinth. The shepherds called him Oedipus, or 'Swollen-Foot'. Despite the injury, no foundling could have looked more rosy and intact. Corinth was a childless court; this Oedipus came as if in answer to a royal prayer. So he was adopted, and raised in Corinth as a loving and a well-beloved son.

Years went by. The boy became a model prince, the perfect son and heir. Then, on the verge of manhood, Oedipus did as custom decreed – and made a Delphic pilgrimage, to hear Apollo's voice.

The oracle was brusque. Oedipus was overcome with disbelief, and tried it several times. Each answer was the same: *'Your father dies because of his son. Your mother's bridegroom is her son.'*

Apollo intended some dreadful and demented fate for him. That was the only interpretation the priests of Delphi could offer to bewildered Oedipus. Just as no one could explain the mysterious deformity of his feet, so it was unfathomable that he should ever bring about the death of his fond old father, Corinth's king; and utterly bizarre to think that he must one day marry his mother – the stooping, white-haired woman who had cosseted him for as long as he could remember.

Oedipus beseeched the priests. What should he do? They confessed themselves at a loss. But one thing was clear: if he wanted to avoid the fate that Apollo had pronounced, he must never return to Corinth while his parents were alive.

Miserably, aimlessly, Oedipus began to trudge down from Delphi's terraced heights. Where was he to go? What if, by not returning home, he caused his father to perish by a stroke of grief? He was pausing at a crossroads, still deep in dejected thoughts, when the impact came. A chariot, hurled at furious pace, came racketing into the junction of roads, and bowled him out of the way. There was a slew of wheels, a team of horses whinnying. When Oedipus raised his head, he saw the reckless driver prostrate in the dust. The passenger, a stout and red-faced man, was clambering down, angrily cursing and brandishing a whip. Oedipus shrank in agony: one of the wheels had rolled across his dragging foot. But this pompous man was raging all the same, as if the fault were his. Oedipus protested innocence; but the whip came down, and caught Oedipus smartly across the cheek. Oedipus had nothing about him save his walking staff: he swung it now, to fend off this precipitous attack. Oedipus had never been the fighting sort of boy; but he was young, and strong, and by chance his swipe connected sweetly on the aggressor's chin. Now two bodies were laid out unconscious by the wayside. 'Well,' said Oedipus, gathering himself, 'when you two bullies come round, perhaps you'll take more care how you proceed.'

Smarting from the bruises he had gained, Oedipus wandered on his way. He felt suddenly pleased with himself; as if, in the heat of this trivial incident, he had somehow come of age.

He did not see the steady rivulet of blood that issued from the head of the red-faced man, who – by chance – had taken a fall that fractured his skull.

Relishing his new-found confidence, Oedipus headed east, towards the Boeotian plains. He was ready to prove his worth in the world; no challenge seemed too great. So when he was cautioned by fellow travellers not to go near the city of Thebes, his immediate response was: *Why not?* Because, they said, it was too dangerous. A monster had taken up residence there – a thing composed of a woman's face and a lion's bulk, with a massive pair of wings. This was the Sphinx and, most perversely, she could talk in human tongue.

Oedipus was intrigued. All travellers have their stock of tales – but this was something else. The folk he met were adamant that Thebes was out of bounds. The Sphinx was like a sentinel of death. She crouched upon a column by the city's principal gate, and preyed on passers-by. She seized and tore them for her food – but also toyed with them. She gave them a riddle to decode. If anyone could answer it – then she would fly away.

'And the city would be thankful for that,' as Oedipus observed. 'Very thankful indeed.'

Here was his chance to do some good – the opposite of harm. He swaggered on, and came within sight of Thebes. The road became eerily clear. The tales were not untrue. From afar it looked like some magnificent gilded statue. Close up it was real enough. Squatting upon a pillar, smiling and preening herself: the arched, tawny Sphinx. Oedipus doffed his wide-brimmed pilgrim's hat to her. She fixed her cold green eyes on him.

Her voice was deceptively soft and warm. 'Young man,' she mewed, 'I suppose you think you know it all?'

Oedipus met her stare. 'I know too much,' he soberly replied.

The Sphinx examined one of her claws, as if preparing for its use. 'Then answer me this,' she said: '*In my morning I go about on four feet; in my afternoon, on two; and in my evening-time, on three. What animal am I?*'

Many honest wayfarers had been tested by this riddle, and none survived. Oedipus, however, did not take long to think. Feet were, quite literally, a sore point in his life. His response was prompt and crisp.

'Human beings, of course. As babies, they crawl about on hands and knees. Grown up, they walk erect; and in old age, they move with the aid of a stick. Morning, afternoon, evening-time: four legs, two legs, three.'

The Sphinx emitted a thwarted roar; beat her huge wings, and soon began to rise out of sight. Oedipus heard cheering. It came from the city's battlements. Moments later, he was swept up by a jubilant crowd, and carried aloft into Thebes.

He had expected gratitude. He got that – and more. Not only had he saved this city from the clutches of the Sphinx; he had shown himself the obvious successor to the throne. Only a few days prior to this deliverance, the lord of Thebes had died: having set out to consult the oracle on the problem of the Sphinx, King Laius had met his end – at the hands of a gang of bandits, so it seemed. Thebes was without a ruler. Would this young hero fill the place – and take the widowed queen, Jocasta, as his wife?

Oedipus accepted. His luck, for sure, had turned. Now he could redeem himself. Word could be sent to Corinth, that Oedipus was prospering at Thebes: clearly enough, no danger to his parents now.

Jocasta was his senior. But she was a handsome woman still, and one whose longings for motherhood remained. She welcomed Oedipus with natural affection. He fell gladly into her arms. To press his face between her breasts was every bit as good as going home. Royal offspring followed their match: two daughters and two sons.

Oedipus was a conscientious king, always concerned to do the best for all. Thebes flourished once more, for a decade or so. When eventually the region became infected by a plague, it was typical of Oedipus that he did all he could to find a remedy. Having exhausted pharmacies, the king turned to his soothsayers. Their message was direct: Thebes was polluted by a murderer. The epidemic would not go, until cleansing was achieved. Whoever had killed King Laius, long ago, was still at large in Thebes. He must be brought to justice now.

Oedipus himself led the enquiry. Laius, he learned, had set out for Delphi with his charioteer, going by a back route, to avoid the Sphinx. But that was all that anybody knew. The next thing reported was that king and driver had been discovered lifeless by the road – ambushed, everyone supposed, by common ruffians.

Did this happen at a crossroads? Was there any robbery? Oedipus was keen to know. The Thebans could not say. Oedipus told them what had happened on *his* way from Delphi. They shook their heads. Disputes over rights of way were hardly tantamount to homicide.

The plague abided at Thebes, taking its daily toll. Then, while Oedipus was still earnestly endeavouring to locate a cure, tidings were brought from Corinth. There, the aged king at last had died. Would Oedipus now care to come to Corinth and occupy his rightful throne?

It was a very elderly man who brought this invitation, a sunburnt shepherd type, undaunted by the plague. Oedipus took him to one side, and explained his quandary. He was relieved, he said, to hear that his father's demise had been peaceful and mature. But while his mother lived, he still must stay where he was. Her virtue was in jeopardy from him: so the oracle had unambiguously pronounced.

The old shepherd's face creased into smiles. 'Your highness,' he grinned, 'if I may be so bold. The good lady is *no more your mother than me*. I should know. I presented you to her my very self.'

What else is left to this story? What pleasure can it bring, what lessons shall we learn?

Here is what befell them all. Oedipus recalled to Thebes the greatest seer there was – blind Teiresias. Could *he* confirm what might be known? Yes: a baby boy had been exposed, and had not died, but was conveyed to Corinth. Yes: Laius it was who had lost his temper at the crossroads, and been left as dead. And yes, dear Oedipus: Jocasta was mother both to him and his children.

Jocasta had already guessed as much. Oedipus discovered her dead in their matrimonial chamber, hanging from a noose. He found this sight unbearable. He took a brooch pin from her dress and plunged it deep into the jelly of his eyes. Horrors would not cease; but he should see no more of them. Then, because he had vowed to banish from Thebes whoever had murdered Laius, he banished himself. Antigone, the child of his who cared the most, guided him away.

Now where on earth was he to go?

He wished, he said, to be where he could hear the sea. Antigone led him down to Colonus, a chalk-white village on the coast quite close to Athens. In those days Theseus still ruled at Athens. Oedipus had not been long settled at Colonus before the veteran hero of the Labyrinth came out to welcome him. They stood for a while on the beach – Theseus and Oedipus – listening to waves perform on the shore, and the shale's rattled applause.

'That's a fine old sound,' said Theseus. 'Reminds me of my adventuring days.'

'Ah,' said Oedipus, 'you can be proud of that. You are as a king should be.'

'Me?' protested Theseus. 'Great heavens, not at all . . .' The worldly Athenian king wondered whether to confess his career of betrayal and negligence, then thought the better of it. What did all that matter now – even his father's leap to death, in this very sea? Water never ceased to rush over the pebbles. Life had its urgency.

'So, my friend – what do *you* hear out there?' Theseus gently asked.

'Nothing,' Oedipus groaned, 'nothing but the ebb and flow of human misery.'

Theseus took his elbow. Here was a man who was ready to die. Theseus was shamed beyond consoling words. For up unto his very end, Oedipus was trying to do well. He held on to one nugget of hope in that respect. It was the only brightness in what Teiresias could predict for him: that wherever he rested his bones, Oedipus would bring blessings to that land.

No one save Theseus witnessed where Oedipus died. All Theseus would ever say was that the old man went with blameless dignity, as if at last approaching happiness. So swollen-footed Oedipus passed on in a secret place, known only to be a stone's throw from the eminence of Athens' sacred rock, where great works of marble were later raised – and where the first great theatre of Dionysos was destined to be carved.

And Thebes? Should we not finish there? Very well. If we must.

Oedipus went; so Thebes was rid of plague. But Thebes recovered no tranquillity. The two sons of Oedipus, Eteokles and Polyneikes, squabbled over the throne. Jocasta's brother,

Creon, tried to keep peace between the two of them – with one eye on power for himself. Eteokles prevailed at first, and exiled his brother. But Polyneikes returned, with allied friends, to besiege the city walls. They were the 'Seven against Thebes', and some acquitted themselves with more or less memorable deeds. But the final result? The two brothers died in mutual combat – quite ingloriously. Creon was the survivor – a sly, unbending, dishonourable king. He ordered that Eteokles be buried decently, and Polyneikes left to rot. The last act of good faith witnessed at Thebes came from brave Antigone. She was her father's girl. In defiance of King Creon's law, Antigone crept out of Thebes one night and laid her brother's soul to rest. All she did was scatter the corpse with a handful of dust. But that was enough. Her uncle Creon condemned Antigone to death: he wanted her buried alive. But she was also her mother's daughter. So Antigone hanged herself; and Creon's son, who was her lover, died with her.

With Antigone's suicide, and Creon's loss, the tragedy concludes. Thebes has served us what we crave: a tale of other people's grief – remote, fantastic, plausible.

# UNENDING

# ORPHEUS IN THE UNDERWORLD

The cascade tipped in upland fells, not far from where the river rose. Its noise and engorged energy were kept in a jacket of juniper bush. But a way through the cover existed for those who knew. Brambles parted to a gully, shaded by some rowan trees. The gully was cushioned with mossy banks that were quiet and cool, even at midday.

If he arrived early, so much the better. He never wearied of the water's monologue; and he liked how the sun was spread and tempered here. It was a patch of the world: dappled with light and shade as all mortal lives must be dappled with patterns of sorrow and joy.

It was the perfect locale for composing his songs.

Orpheus had with him a pouch that contained a simple lunch for two, wrapped in vine leaves – bread, cheese, some olives and fruit; and nothing else but his instrument, slung over his back on a cord. As he neared the waterfall's site a tune was already beginning to lilt in his ears.

He halted by the junipers. There were voices within. Rough voices – cackling, boisterous and loud; making a racket.

This was unheard of.

At the edge of the foliage he saw a donkey, tethered to an empty cart. The donkey flicked its ears as he paused. He saw his usual pathway had been stamped upon and hacked about.

He picked his own delicate way through.

In the clearing he stood upon a high rock and regarded the intruders. They were down below the waterfall, wading and shouting in the pool. Two of them were there: both stumpy, tubby, plum-nosed types. They each wrestled with a wooden barrel, turning it over in the torrent's sluice and spray.

Orpheus pulled at the rope on his shoulder; his lyre was jerked prompt for playing. He drew out a plectrum, and bent over the strings; then let his fingers crash across the sounding-box. An alarm of sudden jangling invaded the glade. One of the old men dropped his barrel with a yell and a splash; the other spun round, lost his footing, and toppled into the spume. The barrels bobbed and bumped away as both men clawed for an edge.

Still Orpheus furiously strummed. It was as if the rocks and the banks and the boles of the trees absorbed and then boomed out his noise. The victims glowered up at him, powerless and spluttering.

One of them waved his fist, but let it drop as the musician fixed him with an imperious gaze. The other shouldered a pair of barrels that stood on the bank and climbed wheezily up to where Orpheus stood.

'You give us a fright there, boy. We's just cleaning out the casks. Here. You taste what's getting ready now.'

He extracted from his sodden jerkin a leather bladder-flask, and chewed off its stopper. Orpheus knelt, took the flask and inclined it from above. The purple liquid that squirted out hit the back of his throat and went swirling around his mouth: yeasty, dark and quick.

'There,' cried his rotund, red-faced neighbour, as Orpheus savoured the new-pressed wine; 'you tell me any water ever tasted like that – eh?'

Orpheus wiped his lips. 'It's – how do they say? – very *fruit-driven.*'

'Drew it off yesterday.' The old man took a draught himself, belched, and slumped onto one elbow. Now Orpheus saw what protruded from the ends of his fustian breeches: two hairy fetlocks; a pair of clip-clop feet.

'No more?' said the creature, waving his plump wineskin. 'This blessed squeeze of Dionysos – made for heroes, men – and us?'

Orpheus relaxed and lay down too. 'No,' he sighed. 'I don't need that to loosen my limbs.'

The satyr chuckled and burped again. Then he let a wrinkly hand stray over the thighs and midriff of young Orpheus. 'There now,' he said. 'Shepherd-lad, is it?'

Orpheus removed the hand. He reached for his lyre, and gently dropped his plectrum across the strings.

'*Her beauty destitutes me*,' he sang, '*I'm a drunkard of her smile* . . . And now, my friend,' he added sternly, 'be off with you. Or else she won't come near.'

Alas: she never did.

It was an accident. Something scared her in the woods. Perhaps the satyrs, he supposed. Or was she rushing simply to be close to him? He only knew she met her death while running hard: too fast to see what lay waiting in her path, coiled amid the grass. She stepped on the snake; it struck her straightaway. Its venom froze her where she fell.

Orpheus heard the hillsides call: *Eurydice, Eurydice!* Her sister dryads raised the cry, and he repeated it. But while they howled to heaven in their loss, the poet disowned his voice. Mutely he saw his soulmate carried off and laid beneath the turf. Then he walked away.

For several days and nights he did not halt to eat or drink, nor utter any sound. He walked away from all the places they had shared. He walked until his legs deserted him. There he crumpled, and laid himself down to go – to go to where Eurydice had gone. His eyes closed irresistibly. Then he breathed, he thought, his lost.

*Orpheus, Orpheus*, he heard the hillsides call. He stared around: could that be her, dancing over the grass? A lovely girl – but then another, and another, and yet others still; some with white lilies in their arms, others with posies of pink cyclamens – all linked in dainty-ankled turns, and waving tambourines. They blew him kisses as they passed. *Come on, Orpheus!* they laughed. 'Who are you beauties?' he cried out, already stumbling to his feet. Their breath had caught him, made him gape; his blood surged to his head. 'I know! I know!' he shouted aloud, making a grab for his lyre. Of course he knew who they were: at least, he knew who they must be. The Muses, the inspiriting daughters of Zeus – born to blend evil into oblivion, and make a truce with care. They had breathed upon him often before. He was their darling Orpheus.

The girls were twisting around him now, making him spin where he stood. His face was hot with tears. 'I want her back,' he cried. 'Is that too much to ask?'

*Play, Orpheus, play* – they whirled in unison.

He got the mood. He hit his strings. The Muses leapt, and he with them. He shook his hair, his fingers flowed. The dance was everything with them, and everything began to sing: not only nightingales, but speechless creatures all around, from all the clapping trees.

Orpheus sat up. Sunlight pricked through leaves above. He assessed where he seemed to be: upon a ferny knoll, within an alder grove. Had he strayed into the Muses' habitat – the foothills of Olympus, or perhaps Mount Helicon? But their willowy forms were nowhere to be seen; only, as he peered at the foliage around, a circle of unblinking eyes. He sensed some expectation here, and saw what it must be.

Tribute surrounded his woodland throne. Piles of tiny strawberries, a nest of hazelnuts; a watercress bouquet; and honey-globules, caught in acorn-cups. Suddenly delighted, Orpheus crammed his mouth, and beckoned to his hosts. 'Come closer, friends,' he said. 'I'll sing a song for you.'

They ventured towards him. First came a pair of sniffing por-cupines; then fieldmice, voles, and miniature shrews, scuttling forward nervously; the boughs above were weighed with solemn owls. There was a vixen with her ruddy cubs; a line of edgy deer; an old sow-boar and all her bristling piglets too. Orpheus gave them a chord on his lyre, and heard its bass refrain – from a mighty chorus of bullfrogs, pulsing under the ferns. An old grey wolf took up the melody, and buck hares drummed the ground. Soon the music shook the leaves. Orpheus tilted his ear: threaded into the strain, a high-pitched piping seemed to quiver through the air. The poet could not see his horn-pronged head, but knew he must be lurking somewhere close – the goat-god Pan, shy curator of the world's menagerie.

They made an escort, and skipped in his path. He told them where he wanted to go, to find Eurydice; they seemed to know the way. The chanting beasts brought Orpheus to a cave, fes-tooned in mistletoe. They watched him enter and disappear, still singing as he fell. Down, down, down he dropped – to the realm no sunlight ever warmed.

He cast a spell, even so deep below. The triple jaws of Cer-berus made as if to bay – then broke into a croon. Orpheus wandered amid the numberless shades, searching for his other half. *Eurydice, Eurydice*: his plaintive echoes filled the dark. Many thousand unseen hands were pushing him along. Did they know where she had strayed?

It was to Hades he was brought – Hades enthroned in council, with his queen Persephone.

Orpheus beseeched them both. He made his case: Love over all. This was his last resort.

'Musician,' said Hades, guardedly, 'we have no need of music here. Tunes, tears – all the same. Signs of mortal flimsiness. Cry and caper while you can – you puppet-shadows of the day. All your poems, and your stories too. Useless noise; diversions on your route to us. You don't believe they're any more than that?'

Orpheus took the reprimand. Hades turned to his pale but kindly-smiling wife.

'What was his name – that monkey-fool we saw down here, in such a wretched state? Ah, I remember now. *Marsyas* – the satyr minus his hairy hide. Here's a story for you, story-man. Our lovely sister-deity Athena once picked up a pair of pipes. She tried to get some notes from them, but they were not for her: she hated how they made her cheeks puff out, and threw them down in disgust. This Marsyas – part of that Dionysos mob – he seized the reeds, and made them squeal. What did it mean to him, how ugly *he* became? Could a specimen like Marsyas get any more unseemly than he was? The satyr made those tubes to whistle sweetly enough – for all I know or care. Then he thought he'd really prove himself. Challenged Apollo to a musical duel. You know what happened next?'

Orpheus knew perfectly well; but shook and hung his head.

Hades continued. 'Apollo asked your friends the Muses to say who played best: the god upon his tortoise shell, Marsyas with his pipes. But bold Marsyas got a mortal king to judge – some petty potentate, named Midas, obsessed with lumps of gold, like all the rest of them – as if that yellow substance carried any worth in *our* domain.'

Hades was enjoying this cautionary tale.

'Guess what? Midas, *Midas* – another fool – awarded Marsyas the prize. Apollo gave Midas donkey's ears, as he

deserved. So much for *his* musical taste. As for the reckless
satyr, there was no mercy for him . . . hung like a haunch in a
tanning yard . . . skin peeled off in strips and flaps . . . Well,
enough of that. I suppose *you* know your place – though you
should not have come down here. Orpheus, you have a knack.
You warble very well. That's all it is. Your songs are songs and
nothing more. They never change the way things are; how
things must always be.'

Hades broke off from his hectoring. Persephone had laid a
hand upon his arm. She whispered in his ear. Orpheus
watched the dark god's face contort and frown; then melt to
clemency.

Hades cleared his throat. He had an offer to make. An offer
was all it was, mind: not for the sake of poetry, not at all;
merely an acknowledgement of love – *Eros, zero's opposite . . .
the force that rocks us at the knees . . . divine ignition of the
world*. Quite; quite.

Hades stated the conditions of the deal. Orpheus must leave
the Underworld, and leave without delay. Eurydice would follow him. When he regained the upper air, he might look back
and find her there – but then, and only then. Was that agreed
and understood?

It was. Orpheus commenced the climb. He was chock-full
of euphoria, exalted in himself. Who said – could ever say –
that *poetry makes nothing happen*? What had this poet done
– but conquered Death with poetry? He sped towards the
atmosphere. With every moment of his flight, the gloom
seemed less profound, the air a little warmer on his face. Was
she behind? Of course she was, she must be there, the fleet
Eurydice – when had she ever lagged?

Orpheus was on the brink. Sunshine promised very soon. He
sensed the ends of roots and bulbs, a flash of petals farther on.
His hectic heart outsprinted him. He turned to see Eurydice.

Yes. There she was, quite close behind. She stretched her fingertips to him – clutching where he stalled.

'*Oh Orpheus, Orpheus – what have you done to us? You looked too soon, my love . . . Reach out, a touch, I beg . . . Too late – they're pulling me, they're pulling me – hold on, oh please hold on –*'

He clung to the blur that he saw. She vanished from his touch: a wisp of smoke, a nothingness; a fume into the night.

*Eurydice, Eurydice* . . . He tried to hurry down down again, renew his pact with Hades and Persephone. But Nothing was all he met: the sullen stretches of the stagnant River Styx. His path to all the shades was barred. He could not cross alive.

For seven months he stayed above, feeding on his grief; retiring to Rhodope, among the Balkan heights. Throughout the autumn, over winter time, he kept to crags and frosty fells: a region where many lives, like his, seemed in suspense. Then crocus-flames began to flicker in the green: the amber-purple flags of spring. Orpheus made to wander south – towards the glades where once he held Eurydice. He hardly knew what drew him there. Some pull of memories; or hope that, by some mysterious grace – or the magic of Persephone – his beloved might thrust up from the cold clay of below.

He never got that far. By chance, tracking through wilderness, he entered a maenads' throng. The women had been drinking, cavorting for Dionysos. They surrounded Orpheus. Was he a spy? Had he come to be with them? If so – which one of them, they had to know, did he fancy most? Orpheus backed away; but his escape was blocked. Their screamings rising steadily, the maenads closed their ring round him, and asked him once again. '*Eurydice, Eurydice,*' he pleaded as they struck. '*Not one of us,*' they howled with rage, tearing into him.

His limbs were scattered across the fields. His head was

tossed amid a river's spate; along with it, his hollow lyre. Snowmelt made the waters fast and loud. But still the voice of Orpheus was heard, unstoppable and clear. *Eurydice, Eurydice,* his call came streaming out; *Eurydice,* the banks replied, all the way down to the sea.

# AFTERWORD

*Songs on Bronze* originated from the desire to create a single, organic narrative of as much Greek mythology as most people want or need to know.

This means a less than comprehensive package. Not every tale of the ancient Greek repertoire is included here. Some stories – such as the saga of the 'Seven Against Thebes' – are much abbreviated. I wanted this to be a fluent read, not an unrelenting inventory of names, places and atrocious events. To select is an author's privilege: for there is, after all, no 'Bible' of Greek mythology; nor any canonical version of exactly what happened and where. In antiquity, scholars disputed whether Argos or Mycenae had been Agamemnon's home; likewise, whether it was Theseus or Herakles who killed the Minotaur depended on whereabouts in the Mediterranean one heard the story told. As for pursuing any historical 'reality' behind the war at Troy, or plotting the precise route taken by the Argonauts, I have gone no further than weaving in some incidental details derived from Bronze Age archaeology.

If myths were bound by time and place then they would not be myths. Nevertheless I have tried above all to *visualize* how legends were formed, to convey the marvellous immediacy of these ancient storylines. Classical authors naturally helped, especially those in Homer's mould – always more concerned with relating *how* something happened than just tell *what* happened. Often, too, I drew upon images from the past – painted vases, archaic temple reliefs, and suchlike. And ultimately there was also a certain amount of sheer method acting. If anyone did see me on a stretch of Corfu's shore, lunging with a stick-spear, muttering to myself, let them know now that this was only the author at work, rehearsing the fury of Ajax.

At the outset I intended to write this book for my young children – with due regard for their delicate sensibilities. They, however, grew up more quickly than I wrote. So I accepted the violence and sensuality inherent in the myths, and made little effort to cut or purify for the sake of modern taste. At the same time, of course, I am no more than sympathetic to the pagan world. If my depiction of the Olympian gods lacks true piety, I claim the honorable company of Homer, Ovid and others.

A single image explains the title. Hephaistos, the master craftsman, is crouched over his anvil. Before him is a large, circular shield, embossed with scenes that strike the eye. He has fashioned many things upon this shield: mountains, cities, forests, strange animals and more; but most strikingly of all, the figures of people caught in all the varied postures of their lives. Embraced, or in the throes of war; joining the dance, or hard at work: whatever their actions, these figures proudly occupy the shield's concentric rings. Their stories stand out. Tapped and battered, so tested and true; stories tempered to resist.

The master craftsman holds his work up to the light. He breathes upon the shield. The figures mist, then shine again.

The bronze begins to sing.

*Nigel Spivey*
*Cambridge 2004*